DOUGLAS IN SASKATCHEWAN

DOUGLAS IN SASKATCHEWAN

THE STORY OF A SOCIALIST EXPERIMENT

ROBERT TYRE

Author of "Along the Highway"
and "Saddlebag Surgeon"

Mitchell Press, Vancouver, Canada

Printed and bound at
Vancouver, Canada
by Mitchell Press Limited

Copyright, Canada, 1962
by Mitchell Press Limited

*This book is dedicated
to my mother, Jemima Tyre.*

My thanks go to all the people who provided me with information and gave me access to files and reference material. My thanks also to fellow members of the writing craft whose work I gratefully consulted and quoted in the preparation of this book. And it would be a serious oversight to omit mention of the contribution my wife made typing the manuscript.

Contents

Foreword

AS THE AUTHOR of this work on the Douglas experiment in Saskatchewan I make no claim to being an authority on Socialism nor do I proffer this book as a searching and analytical study of CCF political manners and mores in their more intricate dialectical details.

My interest in Mr. Douglas and his Socialist government began shortly after the CCF came to power in 1944. I followed the record of this government first as a member of the Saskatchewan Legislative Press gallery, political reporter and in other newspaper capacities. As a reporter on election assignments, I travelled with Douglas on the campaign circuit and reported his meetings.

Although I was not in rapport with the politics of the CCF, the government invited me to take the post of public relations officer for the Industrial Development Office. Mr. Douglas was the minister in charge of this office. From this inside vantage point I was afforded an excellent opportunity to watch the practitioners of Socialism at work. First it was to be Regina Manifesto Socialism, then it became Socialism Douglas style— still the original prescription but watered down and sweetened.

When the Douglas era ended and the premier left provincial politics to seek wider scope for his talents in the federal field, it was suggested to me that it might be timely and useful to present between the covers of a book the story as I saw it of the first experiment in Socialism on the North American continent.

There is no pretence that this work so finely weighs the pros and cons of the experiment as to arrive at a thoroughly impartial and wholly conclusive judgment. It is not possible for one who believes that Socialism is an alien way of life in Canada to be neutral about Douglas and his government. After observation of a disturbing trend to statism, my purpose has been to warn and to work as I can with others who are actively resisting the grasping hand of increasing regimentation. A thoughtful person in Saskatchewan today does not wish to be passive. If to be convinced on this subject is to be prejudiced, then I am convinced and to that extent can not be called a disinterested witness. Critics may save themselves the trouble of trying to prove a commitment to the libertarian way of life which I freely admit and even boast.

Nevertheless this work attempts to document faithfully the origins, development and results of one of the most unusual politico-economic experiments in North America of this or any other generation. The Socialist venture in Saskatchewan toward the Marxist or Fabian ideal state was fundamentally an expression of the personality of one man sometimes referred to as "the wizard of words". Inevitably, then, this book had to be about Tommy Douglas quite as much as it is about his party and the provincial government over which he presided so long and so adroitly. It was only in the final years of the Douglas regime that the master's hand began to lose its touch and his word magic began to evoke the boredom of the oft-told tale.

At the height of his career in agrarian Saskatchewan, Douglas was formidable and ruthless as a hard-hitting debater, persuasive as a pleader for his cause and charming in social contacts. Materially, the Douglas years in Saskatchewan have not been fruitful for the province, but they will not soon be forgotten.

It seems fitting that they should be recorded at their termination by something more than scattered and yellowing newspaper clippings and a few magazine articles preserved in reference libraries.

This book is my evaluation of the record of a depression-born radical movement which came to power on a protest vote and which tenaciously held on to power by virtue of the political skill and persuasive genius of a leader who earned the right to the title of "prairie spellbinder".

R.T.

Prologue

THE POLITICIAN who brings to his public performances charm, humor and a flair for the dramatic is always a bright spot in the working day of newsmen covering the often tedious and dull proceedings of provincial legislatures.

From 1944 to 1961, the Press Gallery of the Saskatchewan Legislature was grateful for the showmanship, fine-honed wit and poetic eloquence of the Hon. T. C. Douglas. Veteran members of the gallery would find the Legislature a dull place with Tommy Douglas missing.

Tommy Douglas gave his last performance in the Saskatchewan Legislature in the fall of 1961. It was not his usual flawless effort. Mr. Douglas was a man in a hurry and his mind was on another job.

When the special session of the 14th Saskatchewan Legislature opened on October 11, 1961, Premier Douglas was occupying his usual place on the government side of the House. When the Legislature prorogued on Friday, November 18, a new Premier was installed on the Douglas pedestal.

Officially, Mr. Douglas surrendered his provincial CCF leadership and premiership on November 7. That day Thomas Clement Douglas took on the full-time job of leading a new national Socialist crusade and the political stage of Saskatchewan lost its most colorful and controversial performer.

[3]

The silver-tongued apostle of Saskatchewan-style Marxism made his valedictory at the 26th annual convention of the Saskatchewan Cooperative Commonwealth Federation held in Regina. There, twenty-eight years earlier, the first CCF national convention had established its guiding principles in a document called the Regina Manifesto in which the CCF declared war on the Capitalist system.

After seventeen years of heading the only Socialist government on the North American Continent, Tommy Douglas said goodbye to the people who had brought his party to power in 1944 and re-elected it four times, and rode off in a brand new car — the gift of devoted followers — to sell his New Democratic brand of Socialism to Canadians from coast to coast.

Mr. Douglas' exit from the stage on which he had loomed large for seventeen years signalled more than just the departure of a colorful personality and one of the most astute vote-enticers in Canadian political history.

The Scottish-born Baptist preacher from Weyburn rang down the curtain on a political experiment in Saskatchewan of which he was the chief architect, its oracle, and now, in the sombre view of many of his own followers, its mortician.

Seven hundred party members at the November convention cheered their departing leader and welcomed his successor, Provincial Treasurer Woodrow S. Lloyd, but with the cheers and the welcome there was a strong foreboding that the party in Saskatchewan not only had lost its identity, its leader and its premier, but in losing these had lost the next election, too.

Agrarian Socialists, many of them pioneers in the CCF movement, stood by at the convention like mourners while the man they had followed with almost religious veneration swiftly steered the convention through the formalities of turning the CCF party of Saskatchewan into a political handmaiden of the union-dominated New Democratic Party.

Plain Mr. Douglas once more, but clothed in the authority of his new role of NDP chieftain, the bantamweight with the spell-binding voice mounted the convention platform to deliver his message to Canada. He was manipulating an old theme, Free Enterprise with a patch over its eye and a cutlass in its hand, but on the deft tongue of phrase-maker Douglas, this hoary melodrama is still garnering political royalties for Tommy Douglas and out-running My Fair Lady.

The gist of the Douglas address to his CCF-NDP convention audience: Hundreds of thousands of Canadians are disillusioned because "so-called free enterprise has not produced the good life: the people are looking for a new road toward a greater Canada."

In the years he held office as Premier of Saskatchewan, Tommy Douglas, like James Thurber's Walter Mitty, cast himself in a variety of heroic roles when he appeared on the hustings to win votes for his welfare state. In these roles he sold himself to an electorate always partial to a campaigner who can make his platform sound like a troop of U.S. Cavalry galloping to the rescue of a besieged wagon train.

On the stage of Regina's Trianon Ballroom that evening in November, Tommy Douglas made his debut in a new role. Good thespian that he is, Tommy slipped easily into the character of a modern-day Moses—a Moses ready and willing to lead his hundreds of thousands of disillusioned Canadians out of the wilderness of Free Enterprise and steer them along a new road to the good life of a socialized Canada.

A day or so after the official liquidation of the Saskatchewan CCF Party, Mr. Douglas took his one-man NDP show east to give it a tryout run on the political circuits of Ontario.

The man who had been the evangelical voice and guiding genius of the CCF movement in Saskatchewan left behind him in the province a body of followers who, in the post-convention morning-after, began to take sober inventory of the legacy Mr. Douglas had dropped in their laps.

[5]

There were those among his former colleagues in the cabinet who, recalling uneasily the Douglas sense of timing, could not help but wonder if the ex-leader's farewell appearance had been the performance of a triumphal Moses embarking for the promised land or the spectacle of a captain leaving his sinking ship, first.

Whether or not it is destined to sink is something the voters will decide about 1964. But certainly in the fall of 1961 when Mr. Douglas was packing up to go away and lead the New Democratic Party, the CCF ship of state in Saskatchewan was listing badly in a sea of economic troubles and financial problems.

Mr. Douglas left the Saskatchewan scene for the avowed purpose of marketing a planned and socialized economy that would give Canadians the Good Life denied them by the Free Enterprise system.

In the light of this worthy enterprise the rest of Canada would naturally conclude that Mr. Douglas, before quitting Saskatchewan, had produced this kind of Good Life for the people of the Wheat Province.

After seventeen years of Douglas' rule in Saskatchewan it is interesting to examine life under Socialism and take a look at the balance sheet of government as it was on the day Tommy Douglas departed to sell his New Social Order to Canada.

To get this picture in focus it will be necessary, occasionally, to move back in time to that period before the 1944 election when the Douglas forces were out hustling for votes and successfully attending to the scuttling of a depression-tired, treasury poor, uninspired Liberal regime.

What the Socialists promised Saskatchewan during this campaign and what they subsequently did with these promises are matters of record and this record provides an interesting insight into the operations of Canada's first Socialist Government.

Tommy Douglas, lean, young, tireless and eloquent, came up from Ottawa to join and lead the Socialist crusade against the embattled Liberals. He brought with him to the provincial arena almost a decade of wit-sharpening apprenticeship in the federal house as a CCF MP from Weyburn. Both Press and Parliament acknowledged his gifts as a debater. He was an up and coming young socialist, impatient to head a government of his own and get the New Social Order launched.

Young Mr. Douglas took the hustings by storm. He ranged the province like a conquering Genghis Khan and his voice was a rapier that cut down Liberals left and right. But it was also the voice of a prophet and Tommy Douglas' prophecies made sweet music to the ears of a farm population that had just come through a long siege of drought, dust and depression.

The words of the Prophet were spoken from platforms in cities, towns, villages and hamlets from the province's international boundary to its Pre-Cambrian Northland. Mr. Douglas promised economic security for the farmer and full employment for the urban worker; Socialism would sponsor the development of natural resources by public or cooperative ownership; Socialism would use the processes of chemurgy to turn grain into manufactured products; Socialism would provide free health and social services and lift the burden of taxation from the shoulders of the people and place it upon the fleshy backs of the rich corporations.

There would be no more depressions under the CCF, Mr. Douglas assured his audiences.

And a province tired of wearing the tattered trademark of poor relation to the rest of Canada harkened to the pied piper tune of the Socialist messiah and marched to the polls to elect a form of government new and strange in Canada.

The great expectations of 1944 were never realized. Seventeen years after the CCF came to power in Saskatchewan, the province was in distress with an ailing economy, a depleted population, a pinched treasury and a mounting load of taxation.

If the ghosts of the dirty Thirties were campaign allies of Tommy Douglas in that 1944 election year, he must have felt their presence again the day he said farewell to provincial politics. Drought, dust and hard-up farmers were very much a part of Saskatchewan's economic picture in 1961.

And twenty-seven thousand residents of the province were unemployed.

The miracle nostrums of Socialism had produced no miracles. The ambitious plans for government-operated industries had come to naught. Business ventures that were to bring in the money to pay for CCF programmes of health and welfare squandered public funds and failed.

The Socialists turned for help to private enterprise but the free institutions were chary of risking capital in a province whose government had early made no secret of the fact its ultimate aim was to abolish Capitalism.

Most of the industries that have come to the Prairies since the end of Second World War have elected to settle in the free enterprise political climates of Manitoba and Alberta. Saskatchewan received only a meagre share of these new postwar factories.

In 1950 the CCF set up an industrial development office and appointed a Socialist to run it. The office turned out a vast amount of propaganda in an effort to put a good complexion on a bad situation. In its zeal to make much out of little, the office sometimes let its publicity run away with its judgment.

In a year (1961) when neighboring Alberta and Manitoba were adding more multimillion dollar factories to their industrial domains, the development office of Saskatchewan issued a news release announcing it had successfully negotiated a business deal with a native of Ghana: a package of industrial promotional literature in exchange for a monkey skin.

The announcement prompted one cynical citizen to suggest that the skin be displayed from the flagpole atop the Legislative Building as a reminder to Saskatchewan electors of how the Socialists had made monkeys of them.

Mr. Douglas would argue otherwise. It was an argument he had recourse to frequently. He could claim, and rightly so, that his government had done much since 1944.

He can cite in his behalf—and he often does—the province's hospital insurance plan, first to be introduced in Canada under government auspices. He can say his government gave Saskatchewan low-cost automobile insurance. The fact that the Government Insurance Office enjoys a monopolistic advantage in this field subjects it to some criticism, mainly from private insurance companies.

The government of Tommy Douglas built good highways; it extended electric power to remote rural areas of the province and banished the kerosene lamp; it renovated and modernized an obsolete educational system; it established free cancer treatment centres and encouraged the development of a university which is amongst the finest in Canada. And being a Socialist government with a strong pro-labour bias, it has gone further than any of the other provinces in enacting labour legislation slanted in favour of the worker. Saskatchewan has the second highest minimum wage rate in Canada, but critics remark that this doesn't mean much in a province deficient in industry and lacking in job opportunities.

Disturbing to more and more residents of the province is the increasing tendency of the CCF to whittle away at the rights and freedoms of the individual and encroach on the demesnes of private business. Compulsion and bureaucratic control are the traditional instruments of Socialism and these intrusive and authoritarian powers continue to creep into CCF legislation.

The people of Saskatchewan accepted compulsory automobile insurance and hospital insurance without much grumbling or concern. These services have worked to the advantage of the populace and the compulsion they employ is no longer a matter of much importance to the majority of citizens. The sphere of arbitrary power vested in the Government has been extended and enlarged through bits and pieces of legislation which, because they were concerned only with special groups and situations, passed into law virtually unnoticed by the public at large.

But citizens were jolted out of their complacency when the CCF at a special fall sitting of the Legislature in 1961 introduced a Bill to provide for a compulsory medical care insurance plan. Doctors and a large segment of the public registered strong protests against government control of personal health services.

The protests became even more heated when the Government set up a commission to administer the plan and staffed it with people whose chief qualification for the job was their politics. In the opinion of aroused citizens it was a sad looking crew to set up in authority over the proud medical profession. What especially angered the public was the idea that this commission would have access to private and confidential medical records and in effect have its ear at the keyhole of the doctor's consulting room.

Professor Otto Lang, Dean of the College of Law at the University of Saskatchewan, rebuked the Government for placing in the hands of the Commission arbitrary power to do whatever it pleased in the area of medical care. The Dean of the Law College said it was the practice of the CCF to call forth a man from their own party, label him an expert and turn all power over to him. This was the way of dictatorship. Once the so-called expert had achieved power and started to go wrong, there was nothing the people could do about it.

It is possible that Dean Lang's views reflected some political bias. He is Vice-President of the Saskatchewan Liberal Association.

With the Government taking over the field of medical care, citizens of the Province have been speculating tongue-in-cheek fashion on what the CCF may socialize next. Mentioned as possibilities are gasoline pumps, funeral parlours, bingo games and religion. It is likely, if the CCF survives long enough as a government, that dental, optical and drug services will be brought into the medical care program. The Socialists indicated this in 1944 election campaign.

Weary of the multiplicity of bureaucratic controls and the encroaching presence of government as an unwanted, uninvited partner in his small business, a resident of the northern community of Meadow Lake, Sask., sat down one day and composed this letter to the editor of a newspaper:

"I am an operator of a small garage and at the moment in order to conduct my business, after a quick check I find that I am required to have the following: a Joint Stock Company license, a Gasoline Vendor's license, an Insurance Agent's license, an Implement Dealers license, a Department of Labour license, two Automobile Dealer's licenses (one isn't enough), an Education and Hospitalization Tax license, a Workmen's Compensation Act license, a Boiler license, and Air Compressor license and a Local Business license.

"On top of all this our Provincial Secretary has now introduced a bill in the Legislature which will add just one more to this formidable list. This new license is designed, so we are told, to protect me against myself, my opposition, my customers and the naughty trading stamp, but it does not protect me from the people who passed this law and the question I would like answered is, what happens to my business if someone calls me guilty and I am unable to prove myself innocent of some infraction of which I was not aware?

"As a free enterpriser, a retailer and a person in business for himself, I would say the name of Bill No. 61 should be changed to the Trading Stamp Camouflage Act and that it be filed in someone's wastepaper basket. Let us not be fooled by the bureaucratic methods which were used to introduce this type of government control. Give us some good democratic legislation in its place and above all desist from these continuous attempts to sneak the Regina Manifesto in through the back door.

"In order for myself personally to enjoy some of the things which Mother Nature provides free I have a duck license, a deer license, a fishing license, a moose license, a trout license, a boat license, an antelope license, a dog license, a car license, a driver's license and a marriage license, with no trading stamps on the last one."

The Bill that alarmed the resident of Meadow Lake was introduced as a measure to control the use of trading stamps by retailers. But the Bill went far beyond this intent in the wide powers it gave to the government for exercising control over the retail trade. The vaguely worded regulations made the Cabinet the sole judge of "acts or practices that are considered to be detrimental to retailers or to any other class of persons or to the public." The Bill has not yet been proclaimed but it can be enacted any time the government chooses. In the meantime, in the words of a Government spokesman, it is useful as a club to hold over the heads of retailers.

Saskatchewan's CCF Government accomplished a great many things during the seventeen years Mr. Douglas was premier. Some of these things were good, some were bad. But good or bad regardless, the price to the taxpayer was a high one.

The revenue that was to accrue to the treasury from government operated business never materialized. The income to government from Saskatchewan's skimpy business and industrial economy contributed little to provincial revenues. As a consequence, forty per cent of provincial revenue in Saskatchewan is raised by taxation. In Alberta the figure is fifteen per cent.

Saskatchewan citizens are among the highest taxed people in Canada. It is possible that they are now the highest taxed. New taxes levied in 1962 to finance the cost of a medical care plan will make a substantial addition to the per capita tax load.

In the 1944 election campaign Mr. Douglas promised that a CCF government would create new sources of income and reduce taxation. How well Mr. Douglas fulfilled his promise to reduce taxation is a matter of record in a return tabled by the Government at the second session of the 1961 Legislature. The return was requested by the Liberal opposition.

This lengthy document shows the government tax structure as it existed in 1944 when the CCF came to power and its status seventeen years after. It is a picture that is not calculated to make the taxpayers jump with joy.

The report is a long dreary list of fees, royalties and license charges imposed by various departments of government. Since 1944, six hundred new imposts have been levied, six hundred charges of one kind or another have been increased; about four hundred were unchanged and thirty have been reduced. In addition, and not listed in the report, are one hundred and sixty increases in court fees and thirty-six new ones.

The report on taxation makes it quite painfully evident that Mr. Douglas' 1944 election promise was a bad credit risk. It was a promise that never had much hope of being kept. The CCF, like Micawber, had their troubles stretching income to keep up with outgo. The pyramiding costs of government services continually strained the resources of the treasury. And unlike Alberta with its vast revenue from oil development and income from a more flourishing industrial economy, Saskatchewan had no choice but to turn to taxation as a means of raising money to pay its way.

There were a great many promises made by the CCF in the 1944 election campaign. One of these was a pledge of "free medical services for all." In a speech at Biggar, Sask., on May 18, 1944, Mr. Douglas promised that a CCF Government would proceed to set up medical, dental and hospital services "available to all without counting the ability of the individual to pay."

Citizens who had not forgotten those fine promises of 1944 would find something tragically ironic in a news story that appeared in the Regina Leader Post of January 6, 1962. The story reported that a 76-year-old Regina man had collapsed and died in city Police Court while facing trial. The man had been charged with failing to pay his hospitalization tax in 1956. And it was the Government of Saskatchewan that brought him to trial—a Government that won election on a promise to provide the people of Saskatchewan with free health services.

Mr. Douglas is embarked on a new crusade. This time he is selling Socialism to the whole of Canada. Judging from reports of his speeches in various parts of the country his sample case is well stocked with promises. These carry the NDP brand but not a few of them bear a marked resemblance to what he was selling to Saskatchewan electors in the 1944 election campaign.

One of the slogans used by the CCF in the 1960 election was: "Support the Party that keeps its promises". There are skeptics who have questioned the accuracy of this slogan. Mr. Douglas makes short work of skeptics. He insists—and he is very persuasive—that the CCF in Saskatchewan has fulfilled every promise made to the people since 1944.

Politicians, however, are notorious for their poor memories. They employ a process of reasoning quite baffling to the average citizen. The method is capable of making two and three add up to four or six and it is extremely useful to politicians who are called upon to account for their promises.

The history of promise and performance of any political party always can stand a little auditing.

1

The Promises of 1944

IT IS THE nature of politicians to make promises. Election platforms of political parties are not unlike the weekend bargain offerings of supermarkets competing for the shopper's dollar. And it is the nature of voters, large numbers of them at least, to give their patronage to the political party advertising the most attractive promises.

The 1944 election campaign of the CCF Party was run in supermarket style. Bargains galore were piled on the party's election platform and the competition was just a little too rich for the Liberals and Conservatives, no mean traders themselves at the business of soliciting votes. The CCF had a promise for every palate (Capitalists excluded) and a premium with every promise. A chicken in every pot looked good to people who still shuddered at the remembered taste of dried fish and dried beans brought in by the relief trains from Eastern Canada.

Douglas and his fellow Socialists peddled a lot of promises in that campaign and when he quit his job of premier in 1961 to become sales manager for the NDP, Mr. Douglas left behind him in the province a great many pots that were still waiting for the chicken.

Tommy Douglas was such an engaging little fellow at the business of manufacturing promises that not too many people in the province had the heart to spoil his fun by pointing out that some of these pledges had been in default since 1944. With his departure for greener pastures, however, the electorate has been looking at the Douglas record with a more critical eye and increasingly the voice of disenchantment is heard in the land.

Mr. Douglas' abrupt departure from the political scene he dominated for so long seems to have been a signal for an armed revolt at the grass-roots level. Citizens have been moved to taking pen in hand to fire off angry letters to newspapers. These letters point up a melancholy fact of political life (Lincoln said it first): the one about not being able to fool all the people all the time. The promises of politicians always come home to roost one day.

Some of the letter writers picture their betrayal at Mr. Douglas' hands in outpourings of very graphic prose. One writer made her point by recalling a trick learned as a kid on the farm to gull and capture a wandering calf:

"You don't set the dog on it, you don't run after it brandishing a stick, and you don't try to catch the rope end trailing from its neck and pull it back into captivity. No. You put a few cupfuls of milk into a pail, and then advance toward it, thumping on the pail to get its attention, and calling to it in soft honeyed tones.

"I found by doing this that invariably friend calf would begin walking or trotting toward me and I would keep backing up, pail tilted toward him so as to show the bait, yet keeping it just out of reach. Step by step I would back toward the open barn door coaxing and promising, and with eyes glazed and mouth drooling he would follow never noticing where he was going until he was back inside the barn in the dark with the door closed, bawling his discontent.

"I have often thought how much like that calf are we, the voters of Saskatchewan. Mr. Douglas has thumped his election promise pail, showed us the milk in the bottom (this time it was free medical care, remember?) and with glazed eyes and drooling tongues (figuratively of course) we have followed step by step until with the suddenness of a barn door closing, the elections are over and there we are in the dark.

"Our sweet-talking friend is gone, the free meal is nowhere in sight, more of our freedom is gone, and no amount of bellowing is going to do us any good. At least not until another election and perhaps not then. Still, if we are bovine type voters, what else do we deserve?"

The voice of the people seems to be much less indulgent than of yore when it holds forth on the subject of the Old Charmer and his government. Indeed, citizens who were remarkably quiet and inarticulate for the seventeen years Mr. Douglas was premier now bitterly complain that he sold them a bill of goods and then cleared out.

In spite of the failure of the CCF to produce their Socialist Canaan in Saskatchewan, farmers and urban workers in the province hold their own with the rest of Canada in the consumption of steak and chicken. Per capita income in Saskatchewan has advanced from a figure of $637 in 1945 to a level of about $1500 in 1961. This income is just slightly under the Canadian average but it is subject to sharp reverses in years of poor farm production.

The farm is still the mainstay of Saskatchewan's economy. Weather and grain markets continue to be the factors governing the economic life of the province. Unlike Alberta and Manitoba, Saskatchewan has not made much progress in attracting new sources of wealth and production which would stabilize the economy and make it less dependent on agriculture.

The blame for this situation is laid at the door of a government which blackguarded and belabored Free Enterprise and confidently declared that Socialism was the answer to the economic ills of Saskatchewan. When this political panacea came close to killing the patient, the CCF hurriedly called for a transfusion of Free Enterprise know-how and capital. But understandably, private industry has shown some reluctance to gallop to the rescue of the province's ailing economy. It has the uneasy feeling that, friendly overtures notwithstanding, the CCF is still honing its political knife to slit the throat of Capitalism.

One of the pathological symptoms of seventeen years of Socialist economic and welfare practices in Saskatchewan is the incidence of high taxation. Direct and hidden taxes imposed by the provincial government have multiplied like rabbits. The average total municipal tax is more than three times what it was in 1944. School taxes have tripled in the same period. The gasoline tax has doubled. Citizens driven to drink by this state of affairs drown their sorrows in a highly watered product which is taxed 93 per cent.

What galls tax-payers with long memories is the promise Tommy Douglas made in 1944 to "shift the basis of taxation from land and consumption to the profits of mortgage companies". This plan to lift the tax burden from the shoulders of the people was not mentioned again after the CCF won the election. Possibly the profits of mortgage companies were too slim to yield much tax revenue; perhaps the companies threatened to leave the province. Whatever it was that changed Mr. Douglas' mind, the burden of taxation seventeen years after he made the promise was still resting squarely on the shoulders of the people. Those shoulders may be a little more stooped now under the added weight of new taxes.

Taxes are not peculiar to the Province of Saskatchewan. Contrary to what many people of that province believe, the tax is not an invention of the Socialists. The CCF simply put taxation to work for them with the enthusiasm of a kid playing with a new toy. Critics of the government have accused the Socialists of ransacking tax systems around the world to find inspiration for the six hundred new imposts of one kind or another introduced since 1944.

Considering their election promises to reduce taxes and the contumely they heaped upon the heads of the previous administration for tax excesses, the CCF have made their own position difficult where taxation is concerned.

There is one particular tax that causes the CCF no end of embarrassment. Like a disreputable but rich relative whom they'd like to disown but find it expedient not to, the Government clings to the province's unpopular sales tax.

This tax was inherited from the Liberals. To make it sound more respectable the Liberals called it an Education Tax. During the 1944 election campaign Mr. Douglas and his CCF cohorts mounted a furious attack on this two percent tax and damned it as the Al Capone of all taxation measures.

Sensing victory, some of the eager Socialists incautiously went whole hog with a promise to abolish this iniquitious tax if they were elected. H. Begrand, CCF candidate for Rosthern, declared in a speech at St. Louis on June 2, 1944, that a CCF Government would rid the province of this tax within twelve months of its election.

Mr. Douglas conveyed the same idea to his avid audiences but prudently made the date of dismissal contingent upon the finding of new sources of revenue.

In pursuit of new revenue sources the Douglas Government invoked new tax measures, sharpened the teeth of old taxes, picked up a bundle of booty from liquor sales and oil and gas revenues and made a profitable deal with the federal government for taxation agreement payments.

Mr. Douglas had found his new sources of revenue but the wicked old Education Tax the CCF condemned and convicted sat in its death cell awaiting a day of execution which still had not dawned when Tommy Douglas pulled up stakes and went off to abolish taxes in the rest of Canada.

The Douglas Government did lift the tax from food and drugs and a number of other items. And then hard on the heels of this good deed, they upped the Liberals' two percent Education Tax to three percent and, in keeping with its rank and dignity, rechristened it the Education and Hospitalization Tax.

On January 1, 1962, the tax was still doing business at the same old stand but with the difference that it had now grown to the stature of a five percent sales tax. The two percent addition was to help pay for a compulsory state-controlled "free" medical scheme which was Mr. Douglas' farewell gift to the people who had elected him to abolish the Liberals' two percent Education Tax. Some Saskatchewanites have been mean enough to suggest that their ex-premier's chief interest in the medical care plan was for its value as a trophy to tuck into his sample case when he took to the road as a travelling salesman for the NDP.

Saskatchewan's socialized medical care scheme of 1962 raises the interesting question of what Mr. Douglas and his colleagues were promising in the way of health services, and at what cost, when they were wooing the electorate in the months before the 1944 election.

Health figured prominently in the CCF election campaign then. It was a socialized brand of health and wherever and whenever a CCF candidate got up on a platform to sell the party's platform the health programme was introduced as a sort of bonus gift for buying the CCF election package. Examine the sales pitch on health and it was difficult to find a price tag anywhere. It certainly had the appearance of something for nothing.

Mr. Douglas aided and abetted this impression when he addressed a Saskatchewan radio audience on February 9, 1943. The man who had ambitions to be the continent's first Socialist head of government said this:

"Just as we have made education available to all, the time has come when we must make all the benefits of medical science available to all without money and without price."

A CCF election pamphlet entitled "Let There be no Blackout of Health" made this uncompromising declaration:

"The CCF stands for free medical services to all. And because the CCF stands for humanity first, the CCF will provide every resident of Saskatchewan with all necessary medical and hospital care, regardless of his or her ability to pay."

Nobody can take exception to this humanitarian approach to health needs. Saskatchewan voters in 1944 certainly liked the words and the music and they demonstrated this fact at the polls.

Election promise and legislative performance, however, quite often fail to match up. The Douglas Government, to its credit, did do some pioneering work in the field of health. It pulled the rug out from under the dragging feet of the federal govern-ment and other provincial governments by establishing in 1947 a compulsory prepaid hospital insurance plan.

The only fly in the ointment was the fact that the pre-1944 election slogan of "Free Health Services For All" seemed to have been forgotten when Mr. Douglas set up his hospital plan. People grumbled a bit at the one percent increase in the sales tax and took a far from kindly view of the compulsory insurance premium they were obliged to pay.

The government employed soft words to win them over. After all, Mr. Douglas pointed out, were they not getting their hospital beds at a pretty reasonable cost? And, thinking it over, Saskatchewan citizens for the most part agreed that $5.00 for an individual and $10.00 maximum for a family was not a heavy price to pay annually for hospital insurance.

These were the direct charges made when the plan was introduced in 1947. As more and more people were hospital-ized under the scheme its popularity became firmly established and no other political party would have dared to tamper with it.

The CCF Government proudly paraded this hospitalization plan when it made its bid for re-election in 1948. And un-doubtedly this painless-payment formula for hospital sickness was a considerable factor in the re-election of the Douglas Government.

That government was scarcely back in office six months when it made an unheralded alteration in the premium structure of the plan. Individuals' payments advanced from $5.00 to $10.00 and the family rate moved up from $10.00 to $30.00

This change brought squawks of protest but Mr. Douglas had a ready answer: hospital costs had risen. And the taxpayers, with no choice anyway, accepted this answer. Besides, in the opinion of most, it was still an easy price to pay for hospitalization.

Then the government of Tommy Douglas went on to win the 1952 election and two years later the Hospitalization Tax took another jump. The rate for individuals was hiked to $15.00 and the family premium climbed to $40.00.

Victory again at the polls in 1956 and the CCF administration took another look at the insurance premiums. This time there was a bit of a switch. Individual rates were increased to $17.50 but the family tax was lowered to $35.00. Single adults grumbled but the heads of families were mollified.

Election year 1960 returned the CCF to power for the fourth consecutive time and in short order they lowered the boom on all taxpayers. The premium rate for individuals was pushed up to $24.00 and the new bill to family units was set at $48.00.

After this larger bite on the taxpayer's pocketbook, the government allowed sufficient time for ruffled tempers to calm and then convened a special session of the Legislature to deal with the business of a medical care plan and fix some new taxes to pay for it.

The medical care scheme was a plank in the CCF Party's 1960 election platform. Mr. Douglas (with one eye on the federal landscape and the emergent New Democratic Party) put on one of the most terrific election campaigns of his career. Raymond Massey never did Lincoln better. As the Great Emancipator of the 20th Century, Tommy Douglas pledged himself to free the wage slaves of Saskatchewan from the tyranny of medical bills.

The results of the ballots confirmed a great performance.

Sixteen months later there was a rather anticlimactic sequel to this Finest Hour on the hustings. The special sittings of the Legislature in the fall of 1961 found Mr. Douglas and his ministers at the dreary task of explaining to a not very enthused populace the financial facts of life as they concern state-controlled medicine.

Some new taxes were in the making. The government needed about twenty-two million dollars to finance the scheme through the first year. It proposed to get this money by increasing the sales tax from three to five percent; by increasing the personal income tax by six percent and by imposing a direct tax or premium of $12.00 for an individual and $24.00 for a family. Corporations were to be taxed an extra one percent.

Citizens of the province, the example of their hospital premium fresh in memory, heard these tax proposals and shuddered. Newspapers accused the government of plunging the province into bankruptcy. And Saskatchewan's medical men said defiantly they would never agree to a plan of state-controlled medicine that put doctor and patient under the thumb of bureaucrats and politicians.

And the man who had stirred up this tempest quietly slipped away to sell his political nostrums in other places leaving his colleagues to placate the mob.

Among the skeletons in the CCF's 1944 election closet there is one that should be taken out and quickly cremated. This one has an odor that would make a polecat run for the air-deodorant.

It is the solemn promise made by the Socialists to liberate the Civil Service from political pressure and patronage. In the light of what actually happened to the Civil Service after the Douglas Government moved in, these splendid pledges enshrined on the records of the 1944 election campaign are worth quoting, both for their comic value and as classic examples of political cant.

Mr. Douglas in a radio address on December 1, 1943,

lamented the awful conditions of the Civil Service under a Liberal Government, in these words:

"In this province civil servants can be divided into two groups; first there are the hard-working, under-paid government employees who do most of the work, and second, there are those who were appointed to well-paid positions largely as a reward for services rendered to a political party.

"By contrast with the under-paid civil servants, behold the spectacle of the political appointees who hold the plums of office as a reward for service to the party. Salaries range from $4000 to $10,000 a year, and usually constitute the chairmanship of a board of membership on some such body."

All this would change with the election of the CCF, Mr. Douglas assured his listeners.

"We intend to set up a non-political Civil Service Commission, free from interference by either politicians or local patronage committees. We believe that the only requirement for employment in the Civil Service should be WHAT you know, not WHO you know."

Mr. Douglas in the excitement of winning his first provincial election evidently got his WHAT you know confused with his WHO you know when he began to put into execution his pre-election blueprint for the CCF Civil Service. This can be the only explanation for the fact that the job of running Mr. Douglas' non-political Civil Service Commission was given to a dyed-in-the-wool party supporter and member of the Moose Jaw CCF executive.

Under the sharp-eyed proctorship of this party stalwart few Liberals, Conservatives or Social Creditors ever succeeded in sneaking into the CCF Civil Service. Political purity was the one sure passport to the public payroll. The service also began to function as a sort of Gentlemen's Club, with honorarium attached, for unemployed CCF MPs and MLAs.

The Saskatchewan Civil Service has one thing to its credit. It created a lot of jobs for friends and supporters of the party who otherwise might have joined the great outward flow of population seeking in other parts of Canada the employment opportunities they could not find in Saskatchewan.

The year the CCF annihilated the Liberal regime, the public service population numbered 2769. In 1961, seventeen years after the CCF took office, the number of Civil Servants had tripled to 7209.

In this same period 234,000 persons packed up and left the province. Between 1944 and 1961 the natural increase of population was about 253,000. In addition, 51,000 immigrants from other countries came to the province. Natural increase and immigration added 304,000 newcomers to the population but the departure of 234,000 citizens in the seventeen-year period gave Saskatchewan a net gain of only 70,000 persons. This was an eight per cent increase for Saskatchewan as compared with 58 per cent in Alberta and 23 per cent in Manitoba. The figures are those of the Dominion Bureau of Statistics.

A favorite pastime of the Liberal opposition in Saskatchewan is trying to estimate what portion of the 4400 Civil Servants added to the public payroll since 1944 came into the service under political auspices. This is a guessing game which has not much hope of coming up with an accurate answer.

The Socialist administration in Saskatchewan has been called the Bureaucrat's Paradise. Like Communism, Socialism believes that the true function of government is to provide more government and more government jobs. In this, the CCF have been highly successful. In so lush a climate of Big Government, bureaucracy has fattened and multiplied itself.

Never before have so few people had so many departments, bureaux, branches, divisions, commissions, boards, committees, and all their auxiliary and ancillary components, governing their affairs and directing their lives.

Like ants drawn to a lump of sugar, the professional bureaucrats—the people who make careers out of minding and planning other people's business—have been drifting into Saskatchewan from all parts of the globe eager to have a hand in the socializing of Saskatchewan and Canada.

The trains that took away job-hunting native sons and daughters, brought more of these ardent recruits for the CCF's corps of planning experts. This rather motley collection of Marxist economists, frustrated sociologists and theoreticians remain hard at work designing the master plan for the New Social Order. Many of them were unsuccessful in attempts to make careers for themselves in the realm of competitive business.

This quote of Mr. Douglas' (circa 1943) is worth repeating:

"Behold the spectacle of the political appointees who hold the plums of office as a reward for service to the (Liberal) party."

Baked in one huge pie, the plums of office garnered by the political appointees of the Douglas administration would provide dessert for the entire population of the Island of Tobago.

Patronage as blatant as that practised by the CCF has not escaped the attention of the rest of Canada. A member of the Ontario Legislature (his right to cast stones questionable) made a caustic reference to the endemic proportions of patronage in Saskatchewan and the press wire services moved the story to newspapers across the nation.

Mr. Douglas' indignant denial of patronage was fired right back at the Ontario Legislator. The denial was short, sharp and uncompromising:

"There is no patronage in Saskatchewan!"

After a moment's holding of their breath to see if their Premier would be struck down like Ananias, the populace for the most part patriotically sided with Tommy Douglas and agreed that the busybody in Ontario had been given the answer he deserved.

Some of Tommy's political opponents were less kind. They were unable to resist the temptation to challenge Mr. Douglas' denial of patronage with some hard facts of evidence. The evidence was an irrefutable roster of political heelers and fellow travellers peeling plums of office in important government departments such as Industry and Information, Adult Education, Civil Defence, Mineral Resources, Social Welfare, the Labor Department, Highway Traffic Board, Public Health, Government Finance Office, and Crown Corporations like the Power Corporation and the Timber Board.

All the CCF candidates in the 1944 election campaign made noble pronouncements on the subject of a non-political civil service. As they described it, it was to be a model of rectitude and virtue—fitted with a sort of statutory chastity belt to block the infiltration of politics and politicians.

A successful CCF candidate named Clarence Fines addressed a luncheon meeting on December 16, 1944, and added a few imperishable words to the Socialists' magnum opus on the Civil Service. Mr. Fines said this:

"I would like to see it made an offence for a cabinet minister to promise or to recommend anyone for a job. Inefficiency and politics in the Civil Service are two things a CCF Government will not stand for."

With the addition to the Criminal Code of Canada of a provision dealing with the habitual criminal, Saskatchewan cabinet ministers are no doubt thankful that Mr. Fines neglected to do any more about the matter of making it an offence for cabinet ministers to find Civil Service jobs for their political friends.

Mr. Fines, a teacher by profession, was the CCF Government's first Provincial Treasurer. He was one of the depression-born band of young Socialist revolutionaries who burned with zeal to usher in the New Economic Utopia and free the common man from the thraldom of Capitalism. (In the early years, at least, the fire was hot and the zeal genuine).

When the post-war wave of affluence hit Saskatchewan as it did the other Canadian provinces, Mr. Fines blossomed forth as the "Diamond Jim Brady" of the treasury spenders. These were the years of the big budgets. Budget day in the Legislature was a gala affair. Mr. Fines for these bountiful occasions sported his famous trademark: a tie decorated with a symbolic horn of plenty.

Mr. Fines kept his horn brimming by the simple device of adding a new tax here or there when his spending tended to move ahead of his income. Between budgets, while his boss busied himself on the home front flailing away at Capitalism and decrying the sordid spectacle of American coupon clippers fattening off Saskatchewan's bonded debt, Mr. Fines was appearing regularly in the money marts of Manhattan for the express purpose of selling more Saskatchewan bonds to American coupon-clippers.

Obliging New York Capitalists bought Mr. Fines' bonds, wined and dined him and sent him on his way with bags of money with which to bring down bigger budgets and get on with the job of eradicating Capitalism and Capitalists.

Too much exposure to the champagne and caviar living standards of the Capitalist class is something a good Socialist should avoid. Mr. Fines perhaps went too often to Manhattan. It began to be noticeable that Mr. Fines was talking less and less like a Socialist and behaving more and more like a Capitalist. Some people were unkind enough to suggest that Mr. Fines was interested less in creating a New Social Order for the proletariat than he was in providing a Good Life for Clarence Fines.

In the spring of 1960, while his Premier was out winning another election with a programme for "More Abundant Living", Mr. Fines resigned his treasury post and quit politics. It was the general consensus that the ex-provincial treasurer had not needed very much clairvoyance to know that the glittering package Mr. Douglas was selling to the electorate concealed a gold brick.

It was left to Mr. Fines' successor, the Hon. Woodrow S. Lloyd, to break the bad news in his first post-election budget:

the province would have to forget about "More Abundant Living" and accept austerity and more taxes. Mr. Lloyd's lean budget reflected the parlous state of the government's finances. Budget day 1961 in Saskatchewan would not have been a suitable occasion for the wearing of Mr. Fines' horn of plenty necktie.

As a small adscript to Mr. Fines' junkets to the money lenders of Manhattan, it is interesting to review the status of public debt in Saskatchewan and then turn to the archives to see what CCF campaigners were saying about debt in the 1944 election year.

The funded debt of Saskatchewan was at the level of $450 million in 1961, almost four times greater than the 1945 figure of $120 million. In the same period, interest payments to coupon clippers increased from $5 million to $16 million.

The money men are not wildly enthusiastic about Saskatchewan bond issues. To make the issues attractive the government is obliged to pay a high rate of interest. In a review of provincial finances 1961-62 the Canadian Tax Foundation reports the average interest rate for Saskatchewan issues at 4.28%, the highest of any province with the exception of Newfoundland which had a rate of 4.58%. Alberta had only 2.80%.

The Canadian Tax Foundation report also noted that per capita debt in Saskatchewan was at the level of $396, considerably higher than any of the other western provinces.

Now to the archives to find out what the CCF proposed to do about debt. The speaker is Mr. J. H. Brockelbank, then leader of the CCF opposition in the Legislature and currently the Minister of Mineral Resources. The date is March 2, 1944: the place, the Legislature. Mr. Brockelbank:

"The Liberal system of financing, the Liberal economic system has no prospect of doing anything else but continuing the burden of public debt on the people. The people of the province are convinced that debts in total cannot be paid off under this system. A CCF Government in Saskatchewan can liquidate the provincial debt."

Brave words, and doubtless they invoked a fervent "Amen" from an audience that might have outgrown the legend of St. Nicholas but which was still prepared to take on trust the promises of politicians.

Although Mr. Fines, like King Farouk, relinquished his title and throne and renounced his native soil, a brief postscript to this recent history might be useful to clear up some misconceptions about Mr. Fines' affairs after he left Saskatchewan. Some people have the notion that he retired to a penthouse in Manhattan to write his memoirs and others that he had entered into a life of monastic contemplation and was sharing his abundance with poor and needy neighbors.

Mr. Fines, after his reincarnation as a Capitalist, became a travelling man and on a scale even much grander than when he was travelling at the taxpayer's expense. He was by turn in Europe, Montreal, Las Vegas, around the cocktail circuits of California and over the border into Mexico. He was next reported in the Caribbean area where (according to tidings reaching Saskatchewan) he was offering to show the underdeveloped countries of the West Indies how they too could attain the Abundant Life. There was some speculation back home that Mr. Fines might be planning a junket to Cuba to straighten out Fidel Castro's economy.

People who claim to have some knowledge of the situation, insist that Socialist Clarence thriftily amassed wealth—some say a couple of million dollars—before he shook the dust of the province from his feet. If these people are right, it only goes to show what a smart Socialist politician can do for himself in Canada's Free Enterprise economy.

Exit Mr. Fines for the remainder of this chapter. He will be back on stage at the appropriate time.

One of the yardsticks we employ to measure the competence of government is the scale of a nation's or a province's economic growth. Living standards, work and wages, population growth and government services are the mandated territories of the wealth-producing business community. These dependencies do well in a healthy, flourishing industrial economy. But where development lags and industrialization is retarded the consequences are loss of population, an unstable and vulnerable economy and a recourse to heavy taxation to compensate for deficiencies in production and revenue.

One of the major calamities of seventeen years of Douglas Socialism in Saskatchewan was the blighting effect on economic development. Industry has shown a disinclination to invest capital and build factories in a province where the government is hostile to the principle of private ownership, where confiscatory legislation has been written into its laws, where labour legislation is weighted against management, and where the leader of the government did not especially endear himself to free enterprise businessmen by referring to the business realm as a "jungle society . . . . completely dominated by profiteering motives, the quick-buck artists and the hucksters."

Mr. Douglas' "quick-buck artists and hucksters" not surprisingly have shied away from a political dogma that bares its teeth at private enterprise. Industry has found friendlier climates in Manitoba and Alberta for its pulp mills and petrochemical plants.

The tragedy of Socialism in Saskatchewan is the jobs and payrolls it forfeited to other provinces. The failure of the CCF to develop the province industrially is a matter of cold statistical record. The Federal Department of Trade and Commerce provides these figures for new investment in manufacturing for the Prairie Provinces in 1960: Alberta, $103.8 million; Manitoba, $59.5 million, and Saskatchewan, $19.3 million. Saskatchewan consistently occupies the position of low man on the investment totem pole.

The federal figures also tell the story of why so many Saskatchewan residents leave their province to seek factory jobs in neighboring provinces. The Dominion Bureau of Statistics in its "Review of Employment and Payrolls 1960" lists the average monthly total of employees in manufacturing in the three Prairie Provinces:

Manufacturing in Manitoba employed 38,261 men and women; the factories of Alberta provided jobs for 31,934; Saskatchewan workers in manufacturing numbered 10,246.

Saskatchewan was a backward province industrially when the CCF was seeking election for the first time in 1944. Mr. Douglas and his Socialist colleagues promised many things in that election year but they made no promise to bring private capital and industry to the Province.

Mr. Douglas had his own unique blueprint for industrializing Saskatchewan and it was not a plan that placed much hope on assistance from private capital. Private capital, in fact, had done very little up to this time to push the industrialization of the Prairies.

Eastern industrialists had found it more economical and profitable to build their factories in Ontario and Quebec and ship the products of these factories to the agricultural West. And Eastern industry was in no hurry to change this established pattern.

Since private enterprise was not prepared to do the job, said Tommy Douglas from a hundred political platforms in 1944, then the CCF would do the job itself. The CCF would go into business, build factories and produce goods, and the profits from these factories would pay for the CCF's promised social service programme.

Mr. Douglas, we may surmise, was realist enough to be aware that if there was little inducement to industry to come into the Province before, there would be even less attraction once the banner of Socialism was unfurled over the provincial economy.

And knowing this, the leader of the CCF had no choice but to make his bid for election on a programme of government-in-business. Mr. Douglas, as only Mr. Douglas can, painted an alluring picture of a province garnering rich profits from a complex of government-owned industries. The No. 1 Seer of the Saskatchewan Socialist party peered into the province's industrial future and forecast the development of public or cooperative-owned factories producing cement, grain alcohol, protein feed cake, wheat starch, wheat syrup, synthetic rubber, plastics, glycol anti-freeze and linseed oil.

To a population with bitter memories of the poverty of the thirties it was the most comforting and encouraging prospect they had heard for a long time. The farmers were cheered by a vision of profitable new markets opening up for their grain; the urban labour force hailed it as the flowering of the industrial age and a new epoch in job opportunities at better wages; the business community, leery of Socialism but willing to enjoy any incidental advantages Socialism might create for it, harkened to the Douglas eloquence and in those dulcet tones the business ear caught the sound of busy cash registers siphoning off a flood of new payroll money.

The whole deal looked pretty good, even to a great many non-Socialists. One of Tommy Douglas' assistant seers, Mr. J. H. Brockelbank, now Minister of Mineral Resources, did some peering into the CCF crystal-ball, too, and reported his findings to a radio audience on January 29, 1942. Said Mr. Brockelbank on this occasion:

"Let us suppose it is the year 1950 and we look at the Brave New World. The people of Saskatchewan have had seven years of CCF Government, they are secure in their homes; they are busy on their farms, in their factories, with their mines and their oil wells. Ecouragement is given to everyone to increase production of all good things which means better living for all. Saskatchewan people know that they are sure to get the best available health services at all times regardless of their ability to pay individually when they are ill. They also know that their children will receive the best education to enable them to take their places as good citizens and to live the good life."

2

Brave New World

It TOOK NO MORE than seven years
of CCF Government in Saskatchewan to make Saskatchewan
realize that the abundance of good things promised by Socialism
was still a vague distance away in an uncertain future. Mr.
Douglas' blueprint for his Socialist-style wheat syrup, plastics
and rubber industries was quietly filed and forgotten after the
Socialists took office.

Tommy Douglas may have been sincere enough when he
promised to build factories to produce grain alcohol, protein
feed cake, wheat starch and linseed oil. But once in office, he
probably discovered that good intentions are poor things by
which to appraise the practicability and economic soundness of
an industrial undertaking.

Nevertheless the Government did go into business. It
went into business with the help of George Cadbury, devout
English Socialist and member of the Cadbury chocolate clan.
Mr. Cadbury gathered around him a crew of stalwart partisans,
eager to spend the taxpayer's money setting up Government
factories.

As substitutes for rubber factories and plastic plants, the Government went into the business of tanning cowhides, making
work boots and manufacturing woollen blankets. The basic intent
behind these particular industries was a commendable one.

They were to provide local markets for the hides and wool raised by Saskatchewan ranchers and sheepmen. The wool went to the Government woollen mill to be made into blankets; the hides were tanned in the Government tannery and then transferred to the Government shoe factory to be made into boots.

Mr. Douglas was especially proud of his boots. With a wicked grin in the direction of profiteering Capitalism, he announced that Government boots would sell at the rock-bottom price of $2.75 a pair, and the shoe factory would still make money.

But Tommy Douglas, alas, turned out to be a poor prophet of profits. Tannery, shoe factory and woollen mill slid into the deep red and foundered. Altogether, these three Government experiments in business cost the taxpayers a total of close to one million dollars.

The taxpayers were not happy to see their hard-earned shekels go down the drain but they were sporting enough to give Tommy marks for trying anyway.

And Mr. Douglas kept trying. He tried it with a paint spraying company, a housing corporation, a box factory, a brick plant, a sodium sulphate industry and four or five fish filleting operations.

Again, his intentions were good. He was trying to do something that would benefit the farmer, the fisherman, the industrial worker, the family in need of a home and the public treasury.

Two of these industries are still extant but their balance sheets reflect a state of poor health. The taxpayers kissed another cool million goodbye and began to feel much less hopeful about the get rich quick schemes of their Premier.

Losses sustained by government-operated industries provoked some rare old Donnybrooks in the Legislature. Citizens for and against the government clashed in argument outside the Legislature. CCF supporters said at least it was a government that was trying to do something for the people. Non-supporters said it was trying to "do too damn much" and if it kept it up the whole province would soon be in the poor house.

A cabbie outside Regina's Union Station put it more succinctly: "Tommy's a hell of a good politician but he's a lousy businessman."

Government in business proved two things: (a) those industries which had to compete with private enterprise usually wound up in the red (b) operations which enjoyed a virtual or partial monopoly made a much better showing. Two in these latter categories are the Timber Board and the Government Insurance Office.

The Timber Board is the Supreme Ruler of the northern forests. It decrees who shall cut timber and how much. The sole market for this timber is the Timber Board. The prices paid for timber are set by the Timber Board. This is the system the Government employs to conserve the province's forest resources. The system has worked to such effect that Saskatchewan has the most underdeveloped commercial forest region in North America. The present value of forest production is virtually at the same level it was in 1944.

The Douglas Government introduced Compulsory Automobile Insurance and set up the Government Insurance Office. No one today in his right mind would vote to abolish this insurance. For the first time in Canada, a government took steps to make financial responsibility a concomitant requirement of automobile ownership and operation. Rates for government automobile insurance are among the lowest in Canada.

Private insurance companies object to the monopoly enjoyed by the government insurance office and contend that operators of cars should have the right to buy this insurance from private agencies. The other political parties in the province concede that the CCF did a good thing when it brought in compulsory automobile insurance but they also take the view that the insurance office should operate competitively and not make its profits on what amounts to a hand-out from the government.

This hand-out includes some nice fat premiums for fire insurance written on government buildings. Some people question the necessity for this coverage, pointing out that most government buildings are of fireproof construction and that the need to carry insurance on them did not seem to occur to anybody until the CCF went into the insurance business.

Another monopoly enjoyed by the office is the business that comes from various institutions which are the recipients of government grants. Schools, hospitals, the university, health units, tuberculosis sanatoria and charitable organizations are obliged to purchase their insurance and guarantee bonds from the government office.

The Free Enterprise school of thinking sourly points out that under these Utopian conditions the village idiot could run a business and show a profit. Private business, mindful of the mauling the government received when it entered the competitive field, watches with some uneasiness to see if the Socialists would move further along the safe, sure route of compulsion and monopoly to expand their commercial operations.

There is no doubt that Mr. Douglas was tempted to push his political luck a bit further in that direction, but the combination of canny Scot and shrewd politician prevailed against temptation and cautioned that perhaps the time had come to make Socialism seem a little less militant and bloodthirsty in its attitude to the Free Enterprise camp.

For the first five to six years of his political reign in Saskatchewan Tommy Douglas was a Socialist in a hurry. It was in this period that the CCF did most of its experimenting with Socialism and laid the groundwork for the planned economy.

But at some point in his brisk pilgrimage down the road of Socialism, Mr. Douglas made the painful discovery that without some help from the coffers of Capitalism the economic future of Saskatchewan and the political future of the CCF were not good insurance risks.

The CCF made no bones about its lethal intentions towards Capitalism. The party's official statement of policy in the Regina Manifesto was couched in the plainest possible language:

"No CCF Government will rest content until it has eradicated Capitalism and put into operation the full programme of Socialized planning which will lead in Canada to the Cooperative Commonwealth."

But this was not the time, Mr. Douglas decided, to send the Capitalists to the firing squad. He needed them for a while longer to keep the provincial economy in good working order. Besides, it was soon apparent to the CCF leader that a viable programme of Socialism could not be implemented in one province. The CCF would have to capture Ottawa before it could get on with the job of burying Capitalism.

So in the name of political expediency, Mr. Douglas put away his bludgeon and pinned an olive branch to his lapel. Doing a fast double shuffle and with the air of a man only repeating something he had been saying all along, Tommy blandly announced that, after all, there was a place in the provincial economy for public enterprise, cooperative enterprise and free enterprise, and all three could thrive and prosper side by side in perfect harmony.

In case his Socialist following might misunderstand and think he was repudiating the principles laid down in the Regina Manifesto, Mr. Douglas went on to explain that Capitalism, like TV Westerns, had its "good guys" and its "bad guys". there was Big Big Business which harboured the "bad guys" and then there were other levels of business where you would find Capitalists who were fairly decent types by Socialist standards. These "good guys" and their investment capital, the Premier hinted broadly, would be welcome in Saskatchewan even if they were actuated by profit motives.

Once in a while, of course, when he was talking to an

audience composed of unadulterated Socialists, Mr. Douglas was prone to forget the distinction he had made between good Capitalists and bad Capitalists and out would come his bludgeon again to crack the noggins of all Capitalists.

But in spite of these occasional lapses into the language of the Regina Manifesto, the leader of the Saskatchewan Socialists continued to do his amiable best with reassuring sounds and gestures that would persuade private industry to develop the province's natural resources and build factories.

The oil and mining companies were eyeing Saskatchewan's mineral potential with interest but they also contemplated with less favour its climate of Socialism and some of the CCF's Marx-inspired legislation. But oil men are inured to political hot spots and if alluring enough the prospects of oil profits will make risk seem worth while. When a wildcat driller for the first time brought light oil to the surface, the companies forgot about their aversion to Socialism and poured into the province to start the oil boom.

Uranium found in Saskatchewan's far north made the mining companies less squeamish about Socialism, too, and they beat a path to the province's Pre-Cambrian. Mines and miners brought into existence the wilderness community of Uranium City.

Oil and uranium production poured millions of dollars of new revenue into the economy and into the treasury. These were years of big spending by government and the future looked rosy. Mr. Douglas, inimitable weaver of dreams, conjured up for his less imaginative subjects a picture of oil derricks and mine head-frames marching across the face of Saskatchewan from the southern grainlands to the northern tundra.

It was a pretty view from the Douglas' terrace but geology and the drilling bits turned it into something of a mirage. The oil play, while it lasted, made some rich strikes and Saskatchewan's production of crude reached impressive quantities. But the drills moving farther afield from the discovery areas reaped a harvest of dry holes and the oil play waned and died. The rigs pulled out of Saskatchewan and the boom was over. The oil towns of the province felt the pinch and the flow of oil revenue to the treasury began to grow thinner.

Then the market for uranium collapsed and the province's northern mines began to close down. The residents of Uranium City faced the dreary prospect of becoming inhabitants of a ghost town. Saskatchewan's northern mining boom was over, too.

Mr. Douglas also put on a campaign to attract the manufacturing industries to Saskatchewan. Although he labels the Free Enterprise system a "jungle society" and likens this system to a cream separator with greedy, profit-hungry Capitalists sitting at the spout lapping up all the cream and leaving the skim milk for the workers, Mr. Douglas now seemed rather anxious to transplant this jungle in the economic soil of Saskatchewan. He even appeared willing to let the Capitalists siphon off some of the cream.

Campaigner Douglas used his cream separator story on several occasions during the hard-fought Weyburn by-election. Ross Thatcher, provincial Liberal leader, travelling behind the NDP chief on the campaign trail, presented to his election audiences an assortment of facts and figures which seemed to suggest that there wasn't very much cream left in Saskatchewan for anybody to siphon off. Weyburn electors apparently agreed with Mr. Thatcher, for this old CCF stronghold and seat held by Mr. Douglas until he accepted the NDP job fell to the Liberals in December, 1961.

These were some of the fine promises made by the CCF in the 1944 election campaign. And when he found they were promises he could not fulfil, Tommy Douglas, too late, turned for help to a system he had scorned and maligned. Then he left.

3

The Spellbinder

THE ESTEVAN hall was packed, which is par for the course when Tommy Douglas is the speaker. It was the election campaign of 1960 and Mr. Douglas was selling his programme for "More Abundant Living". The well-known Douglas finesse was at work and the crowd loved it; a crowd predominantly CCF, of course.

The hard shell Tory farmer leaning against the wall at the rear of the hall took no part in the hand-clapping that greeted the speaker's fulminations and sallies of wit but it was plain from the expression on his face that he admired the platform technique. The crowd roared at a Douglas quip and the Tory farmer chuckled in spite of himself.

"That was a good one," he conceded. "I don't believe a word he says, but you can't help but like the little cuss."

Liking Tommy Douglas is not a monopoly of the Socialists.

Members of the Liberal opposition in the Saskatchewan Legislature who often have felt the cutting edge of the Douglas scalpel, and who in turn have called Tommy Douglas harsh names, will own up to harbouring a small, sneaking fondness for the "little so-and-so."

Saskatchewan's short, slight titan of the tongue, who came to politics by way of the Baptist pulpit, is a charmer. Some part of this charm he came by naturally, the rest was carefully cultivated.

"He has made a career of getting people to like him," said a former Government employee who was close to the ex-premier. "The word 'no' has no place in his vocabulary. He would pacify an angry delegation with soft words and vague promises and send it on its way convinced that Tommy Douglas is a pretty nice little guy who will fix everything. The interview over, he would assign the dirty job of firmly rejecting the delegation's request to some hapless cabinet colleague. It was never Tommy who turned them down."

Part of the success of the Douglas platform technique is the ability of the man quickly to catch the mood of an audience and exploit it. At the business of attuning his message to fit the audience, the Socialist leader is an expert. Addressing an audience of farm people or urban workers he will bear down heavily on the theme of an economic system that caters to the rich and the powerful at the expense of the farmer and the labourer. And listening to Tommy's vehement condemnation of Capitalism, this audience sees him as one of themselves. But then there is the Douglas who speaks to an audience of businessmen. On such occasions the lyrics and melody are quite different. Now there is praise for the contribution made by Free Enterprise to the development of the Canadian economy. The audience's suspicions are further allayed by the declaration that both private and public ownership have a place in the economic life of the nation. The businessman audience is never entertained with quotations from the Regina Manifesto.

"Hell," said one Saskatoon businessman after listening to Douglas addressing a Chamber of Commerce meeting, "that fellow is no more Socialist than I am."

Some years ago Mr. Douglas was invited to speak to the Empire Club of Toronto. He was well aware that his audience would not be a friendly one. He could easily have found an excuse for turning down the invitation but Douglas has never backed away from a hostile audience. And besides, it was a challenge he could not resist.

In Toronto the Saskatchewan Socialist leader found exactly what he had expected: a cold-faced audience of old-line Conservatives and tough Bay Street financiers. To these people the word Socialism was a synonym for leprosy. They clapped politely when Douglas was introduced but the chill in the air remained.

It was a chill that Douglas went to work on. He was not tonight a salesman for Socialism. He was out to sell himself and his method was entertainment. He had chosen his funny stories carefully. He told them well and in ten minutes he had his audience laughing. At the half-way mark of his performance the chill in the air was gone and Bay Street was applauding lustily. When it was all over they came up to pump his hand.

Saskatchewan voters have felt the impact of the Douglas charm in five provincial election campaigns. And it was potent enough to send them to the polls in number sufficiently partisan to keep the CCF in power for seventeen years.

The Douglas charm has several facets, all of them persuasive. Tommy greeting and shaking hands with constitutents makes Dale Carnegie look like a rank amateur at the business of winning friends and influencing people. The engaging smile, the warm voice and the friendly, sympathetic manner have a devastating effect on women, age eight to eighty. Their menfolk may be only slightly less vulnerable to this charm. It has its effect, too, on supposedly hardboiled and cynical members of the Fourth Estate.

The novelty of an island of Socialism in a continental sea of Free Enterprise has attracted Press representatives from all parts of Canada and the U.S. In the years he occupied the big comfortable office on the second floor of the Legislative Building, Premier Douglas seldom saw a week go by without a visit from a member of the Press: political reporter, feature writer, financial editor or a columnist. They came from Toronto, Montreal, Vancouver, New York, Chicago, Washington, Minneapolis, Seattle and Catfish Junction, Missouri.

The visiting newsmen, especially those from the U.S., were always disappointed to find that the Socialist citadel in Regina bore no visible signs of Kremlin influence. A journalist from Dallas admitted some disenchantment when the Socialist premier failed to address him as "Comrade" and regale him with vodka.

The out-of-town Press representatives invariably inspected the walls of the Premier's office in the hope of discovering a portrait of Karl Marx. It came as something of a shock to find instead an autographed picture of Mackenzie King. Other pictures that occasioned no surprise were those of Abraham Lincoln and of J. S. Woodsworth, one of the founding fathers of the CCF.

Douglas is an old hand at parrying the questions of the Press and he skillfully employs a platitude or joke to maneuver smoothly away from sensitive areas of discussion. The visitors usually had to find grist for their journalistic mills in the Soviet-flavoured, anti-Capitalistic preachments of the CCF Bible, the Regina Manifesto.

Not all, but many of the Press people came prepared to pillory Tommy Douglas and his CCF Government, but after exposure to the Douglas charm they went away admiring the man and mellowed in attitude toward his government. The Socialist leader when he was premier handled the Press well. He travelled the length of his big office to greet them at the door and the warmth of his welcome made them friendly to Tommy Douglas right at the outset.

"I didn't expect the 21-gun-salute treatment," a Toronto Star reporter recalled. "I thought for a second he had mistaken me for Lord Beaverbrook."

The Douglas geniality, humour and, to his visitor, complete absence of political guile made him popular with the Press and this esteem was reflected in articles and stories about Tommy Douglas that were usually friendly and often laudatory.

A reporter might spend twenty to thirty minutes with this

genial host and then hurry to his typewriter convinced he had turned Douglas inside out and found the man beneath the politician. Since 1944, Tommy Douglas has obligingly assisted several hundred newsroom psychologists thus to discover the man under the politician.

The man Mr. Douglas helpfully led them to is described in a spate of superlatives that gushed from the typewriter of Jack Scott, columnist for the Vancouver Sun and part-time publicist for the CCF. After a thirty-minute searching psychoanalysis of his subject, Scott solemnly rendered his verdict in these words:

"This man Douglas is—well, how'll I put it? He's a good deed in a naughty world. He's a breath of clean prairie air in a stifling climate of payola and chicanery and double-talk and pretense, global and local.

"Forget the politics. Here's a man who wanted to do something for the improvement of the human race. He chose the method that seemed best to him, quarrel with it if you will. He was motivated entirely by an ideal."

"To call him a politician, as you'd call Bennett or Diefenbaker politicians, is to insult him. He was and is a dreamer and a humanitarian, incorruptible, genuine and intellectually honest."

Scott's dreamer was not found asleep at the political switch when this piece of perfumed prose reached Regina. That issue of The Sun was avidly received and soon the CCF's own printing company was rolling out reprints of the article and rushing them to Socialist candidates in the 1960 election campaign.

Ralph Allen of Maclean's Magazine did a piece on Douglas in the issue of the magazine for April 8, 1961. This was the period when there was much speculation about Douglas leading the New Democratic Party. Tommy himself was saying "no" and at the same time cleaning out his desk in the Legislative Building.

Writer Allen, with the mature reporter's distrust of nickel-in-the-slot psychoanalysis, drew upon the judgments and valuations of others closer to Douglas when he put together his profile of the Socialist Premier. One of these was Douglas Fisher, the CCF member of Parliament for Port Arthur. Mr. Fisher said of Douglas:

"Tommy has become a folk figure. But he isn't the round little gem he looks to the average voter. You don't stay in office as long as he has done without a streak of Machiavelli. A man doesn't arrive at Douglas' art in handling a crowd unless it's a rational process."

Fisher, Ralph Allen noted, was less impressed by the "leftist legend that Douglas is a man without fault than by the reality that he's a first-rate politician."

Any account of Douglas' relations with the Press would be incomplete without some mention of his seventeen-year-long "cold war" with the management of the pro-Liberal Regina Leader-Post.

When the CCF left the hustings strewn with the bodies of butchered Liberal candidates after the 1944 election, the paper's editor, David B. Rogers, donned the mantle of St. George and set out to skewer the Socialist dragon before it could get a death-hold on the province's economy and free institutions.

Four elections after the initial triumph of the Socialists, The Leader-Post was still tirelessly flailing away at the entrenched Douglas regime. Endlessly, the editors of the paper ground out their anti-government fulminations and many surfeited readers simply stopped reading the editorial page. Even the Liberals winced and wished to goodness for a change that once in a while the editor would say something good about the Government.

Good things were said about the Government by Leader-Post staff writers, but not in the pages of that paper. Picking up an extra dollar writing about Douglas and the CCF for outside papers and periodicals, reporters and editorial writers gave away the fact that they, too, were not immune to the charm of the little Socialist spellbinder.

Opportunist Douglas did not miss this journalistic schizo- phrenia. Rising in the Legislature to take a swat at his old enemy, The Leader-Post, the Premier with gusto would read virulent passages from Leader-Post editorials on the subject of the CCF government. Then he would quote from the much friendlier and more complimentary stories the same writers were doing for the Toronto Telegram and The London Times.

"This is the fiction they produce for home consumption," Mr. Douglas would declare scornfully, holding up a Leader- Post editorial. "But when they write for outside publications they discard the Liberal propaganda and tell the truth."

The truth, as Premier Douglas saw it, was the daily heavy output of pro-Government news produced by his own propa- ganda mill. Government handouts, oddly enough, are accepted without question by the editors of the Regina paper. Quan- titatively they fill far more column inches of news space than stories of the type the Premier labelled "Liberal Propaganda".

In fact, the Government's corps of hired writers produce better than ninety per cent of the stories on Government activi- ties that appear in Saskatchewan papers. The province's four dailies, satisfied to take handouts and save the cost of staff work, have pretty well left this field of reporting to the Govern- ment's own Information Branch—a circumstance that Tommy Douglas always seemed to overlook when he was accusing the papers of ignoring news favourable to his Government.

The newspaper Boswells who beat a path to the Douglas door in the years between 1944 and 1961 compiled a tidy amount of literature on the subject of Thomas Clement Douglas. The stories by these different writers are curiously alike in their treatment of the subject. The image they project is one that Tommy Douglas early in his career carefully fashioned as a stock model for public consumption.

This is the image of a David scarce five feet, six inches tall, but a David endowed with the mental and spiritual stature of a Goliath. Tommy Douglas has turned his dimunutive frame into a political asset. He is mindful of the fact that the onlooker is sympathetic to the little fellow up against a big opponent.

Writers interviewing the Premier never failed to take note of his smallish proportions; sometimes this discovery was not left to chance and the writer's own powers of observation. A reporter for Weekend Magazine produced this paragraph:

"The brown leather swivel chair in the office of the Premier of Saskatchewan in Regina is so high that when Tommy Douglas sits in it, as he does every day, his feet don't reach the ground. He points this out himself with characteristic lack of pompousness and waggles his shoes two inches clear of the carpet to prove it. 'Keeps me awake,' he explains."

The physical Douglas is not frail but neither is he Canada's most robust of politicians. His biographers have noted that his face is thin, hollow-cheeked and pallid. This, however, is not the face of a sick man. Tommy Douglas is naturally of slight build and he is careful of his diet because of a history of stomach ulcers. He does suffer from recurring attacks of osteo-myelitis, a bone disease that goes back to his childhood.

Douglas is wiry and surprisingly tough for all his slightness and wan looks. He would have to be for his schedule was rugged. He worked twice as hard as any of his colleagues during an election campaign and Tommy Douglas never stops campaigning. As premier he was in demand as a convention speaker, graduation day orator and official opener of new schools, hospitals, community halls, curling rinks and factories.

By car and plane he travelled from one end of the province to the other to keep speaking engagements and cut ribbons. A Regina housewife, exasperated in her attempts to get the top off a jar of preserves, exclaimed: "I ought to call Tommy Douglas. He's opened everything else in the province this week."

Following a trail thoughtfully blazed by the man they were stalking, the writers of the Tommy Douglas story almost always put together a prose picture of their subject which depicted him as being a man of four basic parts: one part Lincoln, one part Demosthenes, one part Jack Benny and one part that of a Billy Graham preaching social justice.

Government people and party workers who have had a long and close association with the Socialist leader readily agree with the Press that Douglas is a man of parts and attributes. But, say these admiring acquaintances, why limit his talents to the Lincoln-Demosthenes-Benny-Graham tetrad? As they tell it, the Douglas repertoire, challenged by an audience, can invoke with ease any one of a company of helpful confederates from George Washington to Nikolai Lenin and, if you like, Robert Burns, St. Peter, Santa Claus and Markham's "Man with the Hoe".

Douglas' Press interviewers found him mild, unpretentious, gracious, humble and disarmingly frank. One writer pictured him as an unaffected country boy; to another he had the puckish, homespun appeal of a Will Rogers. They reported that he parted his thinning brown hair alternately on one side and then on the other in order to grow bald evenly. His lopsided grin is a matter of record and so is the fact that he is not a stylish dresser. Thousands of Canadians now know that his noon-time meal is a poached egg on toast.

But it was Douglas' sparkling wit and reputation as a debater and crowd-charmer that intrigued the Press and provided them with the piece de resistance of their stories. And after some exposure to this charm themselves, they were inclined to agree with the disgusted Liberal candidate who observed, "Douglas doesn't have to kiss babies. Babies kiss him."

Douglas smiling, urbane, kindly and humorous is one facet of this formidable charm. Then there is the Douglas performance which earned him the title of "Fighting Parson" when he was in the House of Commons. It is more than twenty-five years since he quit the Baptist church to enter politics but

Douglas has never entirely abandoned the role of preacher. With voice and gesture and scriptural phrase he can turn a community hall into a temple, his platform into a pulpit; and his audience becomes a congregation listening to a churchly crusader preaching the gospel of human brotherhood and and anathematizing the political Philistines and those who worship the false gods of Profit.

When he steps back into the role of reverend and dons the robes of the church, Douglas is never at loss for an apt quotation from the Bible with which to reinforce his polemics and lift them above the level of common politics. In a major speech delivered in the Legislature the year before he left the Government to lead the NDP, Douglas declared that Saskatchewan was making "great strides in economic and industrial development." And he went on to say that the measure of a province's greatness "is not just its uranium mines, oil wells, factories or its steel mills. These things are a means to an end and not an end in themselves."

Mr. Douglas' point was that the wealth of a province is meaningless unless it is used for the benefit of all. And to accent this point he said, "There is a verse in the Bible which says that the measure of 'a man's life consisteth not in the abundance of things which he possesseth.'"

Members of the Legislature one year later thought back upon this Biblical quotation and wondered if it was intended to prepare them for a budget which was abundant only in new taxes and gloomy portents. The uranium mines were closing, the oil companies were leaving, the factories had never really arrived and the steel mill was in trouble.

In June, 1949, Douglas invaded Social Credit's Pacific stronghold to campaign for the CCF in British Columbia's general election. Mr. Douglas was peddling Socialism's brand of public ownership to the electorate of B.C. and on this occasion he deserted the Protestant faith to make an unwitting and unlikely ally of Pope Pius XII.

Said Mr. Douglas, quoting Pope Pius: "There are certain forms of property which ought to be reserved to the state since they carry with them a power of exploitation too great to be left in the hands of any individual or a group of individuals."

But in spite of the involuntary assistance from Pope Pius, the Saskatchewan Socialist leader failed to charm the population of B.C. into voting a change of government.

Tommy Douglas alternates scriptural quotations with funny stories. A quick change of pace, mood and voice and Douglas signals that church is out and the time has arrived for some entertainment. The little Scot with his burr still noticeable is a great entertainer. If he ever finds himself an out-of-work politician, Douglas need have no trouble getting remunerative work as an entertainer in the night clubs of Las Vegas and Manhattan.

If for no other reason, he is entitled to a place in the politicians' hall of fame for introducing a new and lighter style in political speechmaking. Even though they may be disillusioned with his government and his Socialism, thousands of Saskatchewan citizens are grateful to Tommy Douglas for brightening up the usually dull business of a political meeting.

The funny story is standard equipment in a Douglas speech. Tommy Douglas tells jokes and tells them well. In his office in the Legislative Building he kept a file of jokes and epigrams indexed under subject matter. There was a joke for every occasion and every type of audience. One of the things that endears him to a crowd is his readiness to tell a joke on himself.

One of his favourites has to do with a debate he had with a Conservative politician. The event took place outdoors in a small Saskatchewan town and for a platform the local people, appropriately enough, hauled up a manure spreader. Quick to exploit the unique platform but wary of making the Conservative the butt of his joke. Douglas prudently said, "This is the first time I've spoken from a Liberal Platform."

Then, as Douglas tells it, a big farmer in the front row who must have been a Liberal turned the joke on the Premier with this retort, "Let 'er roll, Tommy. She ain't had a bigger load yet."

Political enemies, with no talent for funny stories, sneer at this vaudeville performance and dismiss it as just another Machiavellian trick of the artful Socialist leader.

"He gets them yakking first," explained a Liberal supporter, "and when their mouths are open he pops in the Socialist propaganda."

Douglas' gifted tongue on occasion can be cruel. When it suits his purpose he will deliver the low blow and use his sharp wit to humiliate an opponent for the entertainment of spectators who appear to relish this facet of Mr. Douglas' charm, too.

One of his victims was Walter Tucker, for a short time Liberal leader in Saskatchewan. The late James G. Gardiner, Canada's veteran Liberal Minister of Agriculture, plucked the reluctant Tucker from a federal seat and placed him at the head of Saskatchewan Liberals in an effort to strengthen the party's campaign against the Socialists. Tucker was earnest, conscientious and hard-working but he was no match for the quick-witted, dynamic Douglas. Tucker physically was large and portly and his size made him a natural target for the gibes of his smaller and more nimble opponent.

In one exchange across the floor of the Legislature, Douglas drove home a ruthless jab to the big man's solar plexus:

"My honourable friend on the other side of the House is big enough to swallow me, and if he did he would have more brains in his belly than he has in his head."

During the sound and fury of the 1948 election campaign Douglas attacked Tucker personally and the Liberal sued for defamation of character and asked for damages of $100,000.

The action didn't faze Douglas. He teed off on Tucker again: "And how much does Mr. Tucker weigh? About 230 pounds, it is true. Even at that, it's a high price to pay for baloney."

Tucker won his case in the first court and it went to appeal and then to the Supreme Court where a new trial was ordered. The Liberal dropped the case at this point.

After a few years of jousting with Douglas, Tucker had had enough. He quit provincial politics and regained his Rosthern seat in the federal house. He was one of the Liberal casualties in the Conservative sweep of 1958.

Douglas himself has been on the receiving end of some harsh epithets. The handful of Liberals that survived the party's defeat in 1944 were frustrated at every turn in their efforts to function as an effective opposition against the numerical might of the CCF members. This frustration sometimes provoked unparliamentary language. Goaded by the needling of Douglas on one occasion, Liberal member A. T. Procter (later Judge Procter) blew up and shouted, "You stinking rat!"

The Speaker called upon Procter to withdraw his remark and when the Liberal refused the Sergeant-at-Arms was instructed to expel him from the Chamber. Mr. Procter was back in his seat the next day with his frustrations under control.

The Douglas verbal magic has been the Saskatchewan Socialists' most potent political weapon. Party members feel they would have made it in 1944 without Tommy, but they are quite certain that the CCF could not have stayed in power for seventeen years had Douglas not been there to do his spellbinding.

"Thank heavens, this is a big country with a scattered population," a non-Socialist commented after watching a Douglas performance during the 1960 election campaign. "If it were physically possible for that little man to reach and talk privately to every man and woman of voting age in Canada I'm afraid this country would go Socialist in a hurry."

This perhaps is overstating the voting appeal of the Douglas charm. Staunch Conservatives, who still glow proudly at any mention of the Diefenbaker triumph of 1958, dismiss as utter rubbish any suggestion that their hero would come off second best in a public contest of political showmanship with Tommy Douglas.

[53]

Douglas undoubtedly would jump at the chance to engage in public debate with leading political figures of other parties. His modesty and self-depreciation in public notwithstanding, Tommy Douglas in private does not underestimate his very considerable talents for captivating audiences and swaying their emotions.

He would not have missed the famous pre-election debate between presidential candidates Nixon and Kennedy on national television. Nor would he overlook the support this TV appearance gained for Kennedy and the harm it did Nixon at the polls. Douglas is acutely aware of the favourable impression he makes on the eye and ear of an audience and he has no reason to worry about his image on television. He may be better in front of a live audience, but his charm, self-assurance and authority still come through strong on the picture tube. And knowing this, Douglas would be happy to share platform or television screen with Diefenbaker or any of his other political opponents.

The CCF Party's election successes in Saskatchewan were largely the achievements of one man, Tommy Douglas. And this sobering truth was uppermost in the thoughts of Saskatchewan Socialists the day their ace performer left them to lead the New Democratic Party. After Tommy Douglas, the rest of the CCF Government team in Regina look pretty mediocre and colorless to the people of Saskatchewan.

There has been much speculation about the motives that influenced Tommy Douglas to resign his provincial premiership to re-enter the federal arena and begin the rugged and demanding work of building a new party—a party which in all probability will never make much headway in Canada, in Mr. Douglas' time at least.

In announcing his decision to seek the leadership of the NDP, Douglas said he did so from a sense of duty and devotion to the political aims of the new party.

Said Mr. Douglas: "If those at the founding convention

feel that my re-entry into federal politics will advance the day when we shall have a people's government in Canada, then I am prepared to undertake that responsibility . . . . I feel we've reached the position in Canada where the new party is the only hope in the next twenty years of a left-of-centre progressive party."

It is likely that other considerations had some bearing on Douglas' decision to quit provincial politics. There were indications that his personal popularity with the electorate in Saskatchewan was waning and Douglas would not miss this fact. For all his seeming modesty, the Socialist leader thrived on the admiration and plaudits of the crowds he played to and his sensitive political antennae would tell him that his ratings as a public performer were slipping.

Observers of the Douglas technique over the years claim that the real secret of his audience-appeal is simply his knack of appearing to be all things to all men.

"He told people what they wanted to hear, it was as simple as that," said a former organizer for the party.

Douglas is a fomenter of class jealousy. He skillfully exploits the old schism between the haves and the have-nots. Handling an audience of farmers and working people he pictures them as the dupes of a vicious Capitalistic system which witholds from them their rightful share of the country's wealth. As Douglas weaves his spell, the responsive audience gets a glimpse of a day of reckoning when these greedy, profiteering Capitalists will be consigned to the economic guillotine of a new Douglas Social Order. It's an effective device among people who have mortgages on their farms and bills to pay.

But even the most loyal of audiences start to get tired and critical of a performance that has been repeated too often. The once stirring catch phrases begin to sound platitudinous; the sales pitch, monotonous and out of date; the evangelistic zeal, mechanical and specious.

It is said that Tommy Douglas used only one speech throughout his political career in Saskatchewan. The trick was to make it sound fresh and different each time it was used. And he did this much in the way an ingenious chef varies the appearance and flavour of hamburger. If he did use but one speech, Douglas squeezed long and useful mileage out of it.

If his personal prestige was declining in Saskatchewan, Douglas would be the first to sense it. And he apparently knew this was so. He also was a shrewd enough politician to know that his government was not likely to survive another election. And Douglas, after seventeen years in power, would not relish the prospect of being a deposed premier and reverting to the humbler role of opposition leader.

Furthermore, as government leader, troubles were piling up for him. His administration was hard-pressed for revenues. Taxes were increasing and many former party stalwarts were leaving the CCF. Economic development in Saskatchewan was lagging behind other prairie provinces and the farm economy was in trouble. Rural people were up in arms over the Government's attempt to reorganize the municipalities without a vote. The medical care scheme the Premier had hurried into law had brought down upon him the wrath of the medical profession and the resentment of a large segment of the population.

For a man who had made a career out of getting people to like him and thus vote for him, it was not a situation to his liking. There were indications, too, that he was not so much any more the boss of his own government household. Newcomers to the Cabinet in recent years were making decisions independently of Douglas and their attitude to the Little White Father lacked the deference accorded him by the members of his original Cabinet.

Then, too, Douglas was never a great hand at the administrative details of government. Too much paper work irked him and this phase of his job as premier was becoming more onerous and demanding as problems multiplied and criticism of his policies heightened.

Thomas Clement Douglas, M.A.

Platform and audience are the breath of life to Tommy Douglas. Leadership of the New Democratic Party offered him the whole country as his platform and new audiences from coast to coast upon which to work his magic. It was an alluring prospect and it provided an honourable way out of a position that was becoming uncomfortable and a future that loomed darkly with the almost certainty of election defeat.

But if these were considerations in Mr. Douglas' decision to lead the new party they were private ones and no mention of them was made in a farewell speech he delivered by radio on October 23, 1961. On his reasons for returning to federal politics, Mr. Douglas said:

"I need hardly assure you that my decision was not motivated by personal ambition. I have no illusions about the immensity of the assignment which has been given me or the killing job I have undertaken. I have accepted the task of building the New Democratic Party out of a sense of duty and because I am convinced that it offers the only hope for the people I have endeavoured to serve in federal and provincial politics for over a quarter of a century."

Mr. Douglas' rather devious way with words and his facility for tailoring his speeches to suit the occasion and the audience have caused many people to question the sincerity of his Socialism. Business men have talked to the Premier and come away convinced that he is no Socialist, that if he once was one, he had changed his views.

Newsmen questioning Douglas about his Socialism in recent years arrived at the conclusion that he had mellowed, that he no longer espoused the radical doctrinaire Socialism of the Regina Manifesto. It is true that after 1944 he began to soften the tone of his script for his role of Lord High Executioner of Capitalism. Year by year there was less and less forthright talk of eradicating the Capitalist system.

Instead, he began to talk more about a co-operative society

in which public enterprise, co-operative enterprise and private enterprise would exist together.

He frankly admits that the aim of his party in the Thirties was to socialize the whole country and throw out the Capitalist system. Now he is on record as stating that "the best control we have against the excesses of private business is not more out-and-out state ownership, but more competition from the co-operatives."

In an interview he gave in April, 1961, Douglas affirmed that he was still a Socialist but not the extremist he was when his party took office in Saskatchewan in 1944:

"I still believe in Socialism, every bit as much of it as will serve a specific requirement. But I don't believe in it as an end in itself. I used to believe, for instance, in Socialization of the banks. Now I can't see any need for it. Insurance companies and investment funds have become the real sources of credit. If we can regulate them—make it easier, say, to borrow money for new schools and harder to borrow money for new dies and tools to manufacture perfectly unnecessary new models of automobiles—then I don't see any reason to socialize either the insurance companies or the banks."

How much of this milder Douglas Socialism was genuine and how much of it was political expediency, were questions only Premier Douglas could answer. One could conjecture that of necessity he was trying to make Saskatchewan Socialism look less forbidding to private investors who were showing a marked reluctance to risk their capital in a province governed by the CCF.

It is also true that Douglas, when he took power in 1944, had far more ambitious plans for socializing the province than he was able to carry out. The limitations of provincial jurisdiction and the financial losses sustained by his tannery, shoe factory, woollen mill and other Socialist industrial ventures forced him to shelve the rest of the programme laid down in the Regina

Manifesto and turn to wooing Free Enterprise for help in building the provincial economy.

The question of where Tommy Douglas stood as a Socialist was still unanswered when he accepted the NDP leadership and quit provincial politics. The answer soon thereafter was supplied by Mr. Douglas himself when he hoisted his colours and proclaimed the struggle one between Socialism and Free Enterprise. And as he stumped the country for the NDP it was the Douglas Socialism of 1944 all over again.

Speaking in Toronto, Mr. Douglas said:

"There is a day coming in Canada when the people who toil are going to say we are tired of working so that others may grow fat, live in fancy houses that we can't hope to possess and have luxuries when we haven't even the necessities. They will join hands and go marching forward to form a government and to build a new democracy."

The old Douglas technique was at work again turning the "have-nots" against the "haves," fomenting resentment and dividing the people. Only this time Mr. Douglas was not obliged to be a quick-change artist and play his different roles to different audiences. He was re-committed to the way of Socialism and he had turned the full force of his eloquence against Free Enterprise.

Thomas Clement Douglas at 57 was asking the people of Canada to give him the authority of the vote to put into practice in all of Canada the programme of Socialism he had begun in Saskatchewan.

4

Making of a Socialist

IF POLITICAL PARTIES were to adopt patron saints, the Saskatchewan CCF would probably pick Robert Burns as their man for the job.

Though the Scottish bard has been dead since 1796 he has rendered useful service to the Saskatchewan Socialists. There is nothing to show that Burns was politically-minded but some of his work did concern itself with social protest and the CCF embraced him as one of their own.

It would appear that Scotland's great poet exerted some influence on the political career of Tommy Douglas.

The Socialist leader is always in rare form when he faces an audience of Canadian Scots to deliver the Toast to the Immortal Memory. When he was a Baptist minister in Weyburn, the sermons of the Reverend Douglas were a blend of Scripture and the social philosophy of Burns.

It is perhaps when he speaks of Burns as "the first apostle of human equality" and movingly recites some of the poet's more elegiac strains that Douglas steps outside the role of politician and regenerates the idealism that stirred him when he was a young preacher declaiming against social injustice.

This attachement to Burns and Burns' works has its roots in Tommy Douglas' birth and early environment. His birthplace was Falkirk, Scotland, where on October 20, 1904,

[60]

he was born to Thomas Douglas and Annie Clement, themselves native Scots.

It was a working-class home he was born into where Burns
was as devoutly read and quoted as the Bible. His father was an
iron moulder in a Falkirk foundry, an articulate man and
a fierce champion of the rights of the labouring class. It was
a home where on Saturday nights and Sundays there was
much discussion and debate on politics, religion and the inequalities of a social order that made some rich and kept many
poor. And the twig that was Tommy Douglas was being bent.

When he is reminiscing about his childhood in the industrial lowlands of Scotland Tommy Douglas recalls the political
arguments between his father, who was uncompromisingly for
labour, and his grandfather, Tommy, who was for labour, too,
but with the more moderate approach of the British Liberal
to reform. The young Tommy also remembers sitting on the
older Tommy's knee and being thrilled and terrified while
his grandfather recited Burns' Tam O' Shanter:

Ah, Tam! ah, Tam! thou'lt get thy fairin'!
In hell they'll roast thee like a herrin'!

In the seventeen years he was Premier of Saskatchewan
Tommy Douglas was in demand as a Burns' Day speaker. He
travelled to various parts of Canada to delight and entertain
transplanted Scots celebrating the bard's birthday. The Burns
Club of Edmonton had him there on January 25, 1957, and
a local radio station taped his address. The talk on Burns
was so popular that the station played it over and over again
at the request of listeners. The station also sold more than
five hundred copies of the tape to devotees of the Scottish
bard and to listeners who were just charmed by the Douglas
voice.

The Douglas toast to Burns turns upon the poet's range
of mood and sensitive humanity. He sees Burns as a Singer
of Songs: "Flow Gently Sweet Afton" and "Auld Lang Syne".
He pays tribute to the bard's capacity to give signficance to the

commonplace: "To a Mouse", "To a Mountain Daisy" and "To a Louse". And Douglas finds a strong tincture of religious feeling in "Holy Willie's Prayer" and "Cotter's Saturday Night".

But the fervour of the Douglas feeling for Burns comes out strongest when he describes the poet as "the first apostle of human equality." It is Burns inveighing against the struggles and poverty of the working class that makes him kin to Douglas and a friend of Socialism.

An injury to his knee suffered when he tripped and fell on a cobbled street in Falkirk is a circumstance of fate which fifty years later may have had some bearing on Premier Douglas' decision to implement a compulsory medical care scheme in Saskatchewan and as a consequence involve his government in a bitter dispute with the doctors.

The knee injury developed into osteomyelitis, an inflammation of the bone marrow that has flared up painfully at intervals ever since. He underwent surgery for this trouble in a Winnipeg hospital soon after the family migrated to Canada.

Douglas says it was this experience that influenced him to embark on a program of socialized health services in Saskatchewan.

"The only reason I am walking on two legs is because I was lucky. When I was twelve, they were going to amputate the leg but by chance a university medical professor saw me, took me on as a charity case and saved the leg."

The story of the leg that was almost amputated has been told many times by Tommy Douglas when he was explaining to the people why socialized medicine would be a good thing for Saskatchewan. During this campaign the Premier said some rather unkind things about the medical profession, apparently forgetting that it was a member of this profession who without charge gave his time and skill to the task of saving the diseased leg.

The Douglas family arrived in Winnipeg in 1910 and Thomas senior found work at his trade in a foundry and young

Tommy attended school. With the outbreak of war in 1914, Thomas Douglas returned to Scotland to serve with the Argyll and Sutherland Highlanders and the family packed up and followed him.

They returned to Winnipeg in 1919 and Tommy began his working career learning the trade of printing. He served his time at the trade and earned his papers as a journeyman. He worked for a time as a linotype operator for the Winnipeg Free Press—a paper that was to devote many columns of space in later years attacking Premier Douglas and his Socialism.

While he was learning to be a printer, Tommy Douglas busied himself in his spare time with other interests and activities, among them boxing. One reason for taking up this sport was to exercise and strengthen his bad knee.

"You have to be built right to be a boxer," he told a New York Sunday News reporter in 1950. "I'm built all wrong. My head is too big; my neck is too long; my arms are too short."

But in spite of these handicaps and some damage to nose and teeth suffered at the hands of other boxers, young Douglas stayed on his feet in the ring long enough and often enough to become lightweight boxing champion of Manitoba.

He was still in his 'teens when he made his first public appearance reciting Burns at a church concert and thereafter Tommy Douglas was never quite the same. He was ready and willing to quote Burns at any public gathering and he found other opportunities to appear before an audience by taking part in amateur theatricals. Mounting a platform or stage and using his voice to command the attention of a crowd was a much more stimulating experience Tommy Douglas discovered than throwing punches at somebody in a boxing ring.

The labor movement in Winnipeg in the 1920's had many able spokesmen, among them James S. Woodsworth, a Methodist preacher who was to help shape the CCF into a political party and become its first national leader. The

Douglas family listened to Woodsworth's sermons and read his articles on social reform in the local papers. The earnest crusade carried on by Woodsworth and other Winnipeg labour leaders made an impression on Tommy Douglas and fanned the flame that had been kindled when he listened as a child to the discussions and debates on social issues that were a part of his home life in Falkirk.

With the encouragement of his family, the church and friends in the labour movement, Tommy Douglas decided to leave his trade of printer (he still holds his membership in the printer's union) and go in for the ministry. He entered Brandon College in 1924, when he was twenty.

During his five years at Brandon his scholastic record was outstanding. He made a reputation for himself in debating, oratory and drama that was still talked about long after Tommy Douglas had received his Bachelor of Arts degree and left the college.

Stanley Knowles was one of his classmates and friends at Brandon. Knowles was one of the bright young men who worked and spoke in behalf of the CCF movement in the Thirties. He won a seat in Parliament as CCF member for a Winnipeg riding. Mr. Knowles lost his seat in 1958 when the Diefenbaker drive scythed across the West decimating the ranks of CCF, Liberal and Social Credit members in the House. After his defeat Knowles accepted the post of vice-president of the Canadian Labour Congress. He was active in the formation of the New Democratic Party and a strong supporter of Douglas for the leadership of the NDP. He contested a Winnipeg seat for the NDP in the 1962 federal election.

Tommy Douglas partly financed his education at Brandon College by serving as a student minister at Baptist churches in rural areas of Manitoba and Saskatchewan. He was filling a preaching engagement at Carberry, Manitoba, when he made the acquaintance of Irma Dempsey, daughter of a Carberry district farmer. They were married in 1930, the year he received his degree from Brandon College.

One of his student assignments had taken him to the Calvary Baptist Church in Weyburn, Saskatchewan, and when the congregation of the church found themselves without a regular minister they invited the Reverend Douglas to take over the pulpit.

Tommy Douglas and his wife arrived in Weyburn in 1931 just as the depression was getting a grip on the province. The new minister found himself in a farming community that was beginning to feel the pinch of hard times. Dimes and nickels began to appear more frequently in the collection plate.

The reform instinct that had been developed in Douglas since the days of his childhood, now found eloquent voice and from the pulpit he assailed an economic system which bred poverty and depression. The relief trains rolling into Weyburn to dispense food and clothing to needy citizens and farmers affronted him and although he rolled up his sleeves and pitched in to help unload the cars, his indignation boiled over from the pulpit in denunciation of a social order which provided degrading hand-outs instead of jobs.

Members of his congregation of those years agree that the Reverend Douglas was not quite like other ministers they had been used to.

"He took quotations from the Bible but he tailored them to fit the conditions of the 1930's, a former resident of Weyburn recalled. "He preached a practical sort of Christianity that everybody understood because it was down to earth and it took heed of our physical needs as well as our spiritual."

In normal times some of Tommy Douglas' sermons might have clashed with the political loyalties of members of his congregation but the depression had turned even staunch Conservatives and Liberals a little sour on government and politicians.

In the first year or two of his ministry at Weyburn the Reverend Douglas conducted a crusade for a better way of life but he showed no particular interest in becoming directly involved in politics. He was studying at home to earn his

Master of Arts degree and he expressed an ambition to do more work in the field of sociology.

In 1933 he received his Master of Arts degree extra-murally from McMaster University in Hamilton, Ontario, for a thesis on social hygiene and public health. Then he took time off from his ministerial duties in Weyburn to enroll for post-graduate work in sociology at the University of Chicago.

It was an experience among the unemployed in Chicago, Douglas claims, that turned his thoughts definitely in the direc-tion of politics. Mr. Douglas is one of those rare and fortunate politicians who seem never to do things out of plain selfish interest—always in the background of his decisions and judg-ments he can point to the influence of some human experience which makes his motives respectable and even altruistic.

The Baptist minister from Weyburn talked to jobless, home-less men crowding a Chicago dump for the comfort of the warm ashes piled there. He was appalled by the suffering he witnessed in the depression-stricken city and he left Chicago more certain than ever that Socialism was the cure for the ills of the world.

"Conditions in Chicago convinced me that one day I would have to leave the church for politics," is the explanation Tommy Douglas gives for his transition from pastor to politician. "I felt then something practical had to be done to better the lot of the unemployed. Preaching moral and spiritual values from the pulpit was not enough."

Douglas made his first bid for political office in 1934. It was a provincial election and with the encouragement of J. S. Woodsworth he went into the fray as the Farmer-Labour candidate for Weyburn. M. J. Coldwell, a Regina school principal and city alderman who was to become national leader of the CCF after Woodsworth, joined him to contest a Regina seat for the Farmer-Labor Party—which was soon to abandon this name in favour of Cooperative Commonwealth Federation.

During the 1934 campaign preacher Douglas and politi-cian Douglas sometimes had difficulty keeping one job separate from the other. After a week on the hustings the Reverend Douglas returned to his pulpit on Sunday and more often than not what his congregation heard was a political speech instead of a sermon.

Liberals and Conservatives who had been tolerant of their minister's Socialistic views before he entered politics, now began to mutter and complain and a few quit the church. Taking the hint, pastor Douglas softened his politicking from the pulpit and bore down heavily on the good, safe Biblical theme of loving one's neighbor. Mondays he was on the campaign road again committing verbal mayhem on his oppo-nents and contriving to bring about their political destruction.

Devout Baptists found this Jekyll and Hyde behaviour offen-sive. It was not fitting, they felt, for a minister to preach brotherly love on Sunday and then mock the Biblical injunction each of the other six days of the week.

Tommy Douglas lost the 1934 election to Liberal H. E. Eaglesham, a widely known and respected family doctor who had ministered to city and rural people for many years. He was a tough candidate to beat and there was no discredit to Douglas in losing.

It was the last election he was to lose in the twenty-five years he sat, first in the House of Commons and then in the Saskatchewan Legislature.

The year after he was defeated in the provincial elections he ran for the federal house as CCF candidate for Weyburn and was elected. Douglas says he was not too interested in trying politics again after his 1934 defeat but when a superintendent of churches warned him that he would never serve in the church again if he ran under the CCF banner it got Douglas' dander up and he offered himself as a candidate.

Citizens of Weyburn who remember that campaign declare that the election was won for Douglas when the sitting member,

Liberal Ed. Young, a farmer, unwisely accepted Douglas' challenge to a debate in the Weyburn Rink.

It was a slaughter. The eloquence and razor wit of Douglas demolished his less articulate opponent. The "Fighting Parson" put Socialism through its paces and with its promise of abundance after famine it looked much more appealing to the crowd in the rink than a government with a depression on its record.

The 1935 campaign was rough and rugged all the way through and it brought out the pugnacious streak in Douglas. He tells the story of one stormy meeting in a country town and the attempt of a rowdy element to chase him off the platform. Douglas picked up a water pitcher, shattered it on the speaker's table, selected a fragment with a sharp cutting edge and dared his tormentors to come on.

Douglas went to Ottawa as a CCF member but he was equally qualified to sit as representative of Social Credit. The Socreds endorsed him as their candidate in the 1935 election, too. A handbill issued during the campaign reproduced a telegram that had been dispatched to Mr. Douglas on September 30, 1935. The wire, signed by H. W. Arnold, Social Credit Provincial Organizer, Saskatoon, read:

"Rev. T. C. Douglas, Weyburn, Sask.

This will confirm endorsation of convention held Weyburn, twenty-eighth, of you as Social Credit candidate."

Apparently the CCF and the Social Creditors had merged their resources in Weyburn to elect Douglas. The handbill was issued over the authority of the "CCF-Social Credit, Weyburn Federal Constituency."

The Communists of Weyburn were in there pitching for Douglas, too. Mr. Douglas, however, has said publicly on a number of occasions that he neither invites nor wants the support of the Communists. This cavalier attitude on the part of Douglas vexed provincial Communist Leader Nelson Clarke and induced him to write a letter which appeared in the Regina Leader-Post of November 1, 1946:

"I see that Premier Douglas is telling the electors of Portage la Prairie that the CCF does not want any help from the Labor-Progressive Party. Perhaps he has forgotten that he himself climbed the first rung of the ladder to political success with the very active and devoted help of the Communists of Weyburn constituency in 1935, and that he was only too glad to get all the aid he could in a hotly contested election.

"Despite all differences the LPP will continue to seek united action with the members of the CCF in the struggle against monopoly Capitalism. Our appeal for such unity will not be feared by those in the CCF who honestly desire a new social order."

So with the blessings of the CCF, Social Credit and the Communists, Tommy Douglas arrived in Ottawa and for the next nine years his voice was heard often and eloquently in the House of Commons preaching the gospel of Socialism.

Douglas sat in the House with old friends M. J. Coldwell and J. S. Woodsworth, then national leader of the CCF party. The CCF formed only a small splinter group in Parliament but although they were weak numerically they were formidable in debate and the Liberal government of those years treated them with respect. Government members were especially wary of the cutting tongue of the cocky young member from Weyburn.

The late Austin F. Cross, a veteran member of the Parliamentary Press Gallery, said of Douglas in 1944:

"In debate, Douglas is terrific. A Master of Arts, he reveals his background when least expected. I have seen him tackle the formidable Minister of the Navy, Hon. Angus L. MacDonald, and flatten him. I have seen him push the Hon. Thomas Crerar around piteously. The Cabinet he loves to joust with and he is scared of nobody or nothing except Prime Minister King. I have never seen him try any fancy stuff with the P.M., who of course, although it is little known, is the best handler of hecklers in the Commons. Douglas is too smart to out-reach himself."

Douglas tangled on numerous occasions with the redoubtable James G. Gardiner, Minister of Agriculture. Once when the Weyburn member was speaking on agriculture, Mr. Gardiner snapped: "What do you know about farming—you're not a farmer."

"I never laid an egg either," Douglas retorted, "but I know more about making an omelette than a hen does."

Douglas' quickness with the wisecrack was not appreciated by all the Parliamentarians. In the opinion of some, the ebullient young man from Weyburn was a bit of a smart alec and a show-off. Members given to long silences in the House and who perhaps were a little envious of more vocal colleagues, considered Tommy Douglas a gabby young upstart with an artful talent for getting himself mentioned in the papers.

Canada's preparation for war and the country's war effort provided Douglas with a stage and a spotlight from which to deliver some of his most sparkling and moving orations. With war and sacrifice as his backdrop, he employed two themes straight out of his party's political philosophy but which with the Douglas eloquence at work soared above the earthly level of partisan politics and rang with a patriotism that would have shamed Barbara Frietchie.

The Douglas wartime speech predictably brought on stage a favourite hero and a familiar villain of the Socialists. Mr. Douglas lauded the courage and sacrifice of the common people and denounced big business for profiteering on war contracts.

In the debate on the War Appropriation Bill, May 23, 1940, Mr. Douglas heaped scorn on the profiteers:

"I say, shame on any group of men who in Canada's hour of Gethsemane are not prepared to give their time, their industry and their machinery of production towards the cause of defending democracy in the world."

After punishing the profiteers, Mr. Douglas paid his respects to Canada's young men in uniform and urged the government to do something for them when the war ended:

"One year ago young men could be seen riding the rods on freight trains across Canada. Today hundreds are in His Majesty's uniform. Most of us know some of these young men personally. These men are going to fight for a society that could not even give them a job. What do we propose to do with them when they come back? Do we propose to put them back on the rods? God forbid."

In a moving finale to his speech in the House of Commons that wartime May day in 1940, Mr. Douglas said:

"May I say this as I sit down. We all recognize that this is a black hour. There is very little use in the Pollyanna type of optimism. Most of us remember March of 1918. At that time I was a boy thirteen years of age. I stood on Buchanan street in Glasgow in a drizzling rain, together with hundreds of other people. Soldiers of the Canadian Corps who spent their leave in Glasgow will remember the Maple Leaf building. There was a great map, on which were flags denoting the various armies' lines. On this particular morning to which I refer there was a gap in the lines; the bulletin announced that an entire British army had been wiped out and that the German military machine was on its way to Paris. That was probably the blackest day in the history of Great Britain, until this moment. There was not a sound, although there were hundreds upon hundreds of people in that crowd. Suddenly someone in front began to sing, and those Scottish workers, together with soldiers from every corner of the British Commonwealth, taking off their hats, stood in the drizzling rain and sang:

> O God, our help in ages past,
> Our hope for years to come.

"As I looked around at those people I came to realize something of the inner resources that have made the British

[71]

people great in the hour of danger, and that strength is still with us. My plea, Mr. Speaker, is: with firm faith in the 'divinity that shapes our ends, rough-hew them how we will'; with confidence in each other and with firm determination to do the right as we see it, let us, the Canadian people stand shoulder to shoulder in this grim hour until at last the blackness of the night shall give way to the promise of a better day."

These were fine sentiments and many Canadians read them with pleasure and pride and applauded Tommy Douglas for his splendid patriotism and the grandeur of his prose. And if members of Parliament seemed less moved by Tommy's speech that day it may have been because they were remembering while he spoke that this same speaker had persistently opposed the passage of increased appropriations for national defence in the two years just preceding the outbreak of war. Mr. Douglas had intimated, with his fine flair for sarcasm, that the government members were a bunch of old women, fearful of enemies that did not exist. Said the member for Weyburn (Hansard, 1937, pp 1059 and 1063):

"Against whom are we arming? What potential aggressor is more aggressive today? Oh, I know that bogeymen have been trotted out in this chamber. It has been suggested that it might be Italy, it might be Germany, it might be Japan."

Tommy Douglas was a better prophet than he intended. The CCF group in Commons was still opposing the government's preparations for national defence when Germany marched, joined soon by Italy and then Japan.

The member for Weyburn not only showed himself to be poorly informed on the international situation but he also miscued badly in gauging public opinion when he took the pacifist line in Parliament. Douglas opposed an appropriation of $150,000 for cadet training and suggested that it be used instead for boy scout work. The CCF group in the House moved "that the item of $50,000 for Cadet Services be reduced to $1." When war came in 1939 the cadet movement proved its value as a source of disciplined and partly trained men for the Armed Forces.

The free world had good reason to bless the foresight of the Canadian Government in making provision for the expansion of the Royal Canadian Air Force in the years just before war. These facilities and trained personnel became the foundation upon which Canada built its great Commonwealth Air Training Plan—a contribution that did much to turn the tide of war against Hitler.

Mr. Douglas rose in the House on May 8, 1936, to register a protest when the government sought passage of an estimate to provide buildings at Trenton, Ontario, for the R.C.A.F. The Weyburn member expressed the opinion that the money could be used in better ways. Three years after Mr. Douglas put these words on the record Trenton was beginning to function as one of the key centres in the Air Training Plan.

Still reading the signals wrong on the country's reaction to war, Douglas and his CCF colleagues proposed that Canada's participation in the war effort should be limited to home defence. In September, 1939, Mr. M. J. Coldwell made this statement:

". . . Canada should be prepared to defend her own shores, but her assistance overseas should be limited to economic aid and must not include conscription of man power or the sending of any expeditionary force."

The CCF group moved an amendment to the War Appropriation Bill that would have prevented Canada from sending forces overseas. Prime Minister King pointed out that, if the amendment carried, it would make it difficult for Canada to co-operate even in the defence of Newfoundland or the islands of St. Pierre and Miquelon and this would endanger the security of Canada's Atlantic coast. On a vote, the CCF amendment was defeated.

When it finally dawned on Mr. Douglas and his associates

that public opinion was on the side of an "all out" war effort, the Socialists tossed in the sponge and threw their full weight behind the national effort. In fact, it was not long before the CCF group in the House of Commons was pressing the government to put more steam behind Canada's war effort.

Tommy Douglas says he is neither a pacifist nor a neutralist. He put on a uniform in the last war and was preparing to go overseas with the second Battalion of the South Saskatchewan Regiment when his old leg trouble flared up and he was discharged.

It has not always been clear where he stands on foreign policy. His public utterances seem to lean towards the doctrine of the nationalist and the neutralist. He is distrustful of military alliances. He frowns on NORAD and he is cool towards NATO. He is opposed to Canada's use of nuclear weapons. But he supports the principle of the United Nations.

When the Saskatchewan CCF in 1951 advocated recognition of Communist China it was criticized. Mr. Douglas answered this criticism in a speech in the Saskatchewan Legislature on February 7, 1951. He pointed out that Great Britain recognized China; that India recognized China; that David Crowe, a Liberal MP for one of the Toronto ridings, had spoken in favor of recognizing Red China.

Said Mr. Douglas:

"Now, Mr. Speaker, I believe that the people of Canada and the people of Saskatchewan want peace. We also want freedom. I don't believe in peace at any price, but I do believe in justice at any cost. If we are going to have to fight a war, then we want to fight a war for things that are worthwhile. I don't want to see the young men of this country fight a war merely to reimpose Chiang-Kai-Shek on the Chinese people, or to protect the holdings of the Standard Oil Company. I am saying, therefore, that this is not the time to question the loyalty of everyone who doesn't stand up and yell 'hip hip hurray' every time (General) MacArthur, who seems to suffer from delusions of grandeur, and some other firebrand, calls for military action . . . I don't think it is proper to label such people as being Communists or subversive. I think this is the time to recognize that we are in the process of building a world community; that we are in the process of trying to establish world justice, a world court, a world police force, but in the process of establishing that we mustn't allow any nation or any small group of nations to use the international police force to try to fasten discredited dictators upon the people of the world."

With his quick instinct for making news, Douglas in 1943 stood up in the House of Commons to voice his opposition to the Yalta and Tcheran Pacts. He was criticized for making these remarks at a time when Canada had an Anglo-Soviet Friendship League.

Said Douglas: "I was called a doctrinaire Socialist by those on the right and a Fascist by those on the extreme left because I took the position that the great powers had no right to sit down and divide up the world like a pie."

When the CCF in Saskatchewan had softened up the Liberals in the 1944 election campaign they invited Tommy Douglas to come up and administer the coup de grace. The firebrand from Weyburn left Ottawa in May, 1944, to make his successful bid for the premiership of Saskatchewan.

Then began a new political career and one that was often turbulent, a quiet home life and the raising of two daughters, Joan, who took up nursing as a career, and Shirley who married into a family of Capitalists—the Sicks of Seattle who made their fortunes manufacturing beer. Shirley, with roles in stage and television productions, made her movie debut in a film version of "Lolita". But her father didn't get a chance to see the picture in Saskatchewan. His government film censor banned it.

The year Tommy Douglas set out to socialize Saskatchewan and abolish Capitalism, a profile on the new premier appeared in Maclean's Magazine written by Bruce Hutchison. On Douglas' performance in Parliament, Hutchison said:

"He fought as he had fought in the amateur boxing ring in Manitoba, where he held the amateur light-weight championship — fought with sudden, quick punches, rapid footwork and, above all, with courage. He did not make himself popular in Parliament but he made himself heard and, at times, he could penetrate even the rhinoceros skin of the government. He left in Ottawa no body of political philosophy, no deep impact on events, but he had learned the business of politics."

But Douglas did make a deep impact on events in Saskatchewan and the reverberations of that impact were still being felt after Tommy Douglas left the province to campaign for another seat in the House of Commons.

5

The Seed and the Soil

TOMMY DOUGLAS was a boy in Scotland growing up on a diet of porridge, polemics and Burns' poetry while in another part of the world the seeds of discontent were being sown that would germinate and develop years later into a Socialist movement which he would lead to victory at the polls.

The Scottish boy who was being nurtured on a gospel of social reform had no inkling then of the role he would play in an agrarian revolt that would come thirty-five years in the future and in a place forty-five hundred miles from his home in Falkirk.

The genealogical tree of the Cooperative Commonwealth Federation (CCF) is the history of a succession of militant but short-lived protest movements which grew out of the economic problems of pioneer agriculture in the wheat belt of the Canadian West.

The CCF Party might have passed quickly into oblivion like the radical movements before it, had it not been for the onset of a long and devastating depression. This was the arid and eroded soil that nourished the seeds of discontent and propagated resentment against the government in power. And resolve hardened to bring about change through political action.

In this climate of desolation and poverty, the farm population of Saskatchewan was receptive to the remedies Socialism proposed as a cure for the economic ills of the province. The

CCF (and its immediate predecessor the Farmer-Labor move-ment) recognized that conditions would never be more propiti-ous for their advance to power. Through the Thirties they pushed their campaign hard. This CCF leaflet made its appear-ance in rural areas during the 1934 provincial election:

"Do not be misled by false and malicious propaganda spread at your expense by the Liberal and Conservative parties about the Farmer-Labor (CCF) movement.

"There is no difference between the Liberal and Conservative parties. They are nothing but servants of the money lord-bankers and the financial magnates. They want power to carry on the collecting of money for their masters and thereby further impoverish you. They have exploited the people of Canada and its resources. They have forever mortgaged your homes, your farms, and your future to the financiers and the Capitalists.

VOTE FOR A NEW DEAL

"Canada is on the verge of total collapse. Save Saskatchewan from the curse of either Fascism or Communism."

The Socialists had high hopes of winning the 1934 election but the farmers were not quite ready yet to abandon their traditional support of the old line parties. Nevertheless the CCF elected five members to the Legislature and displaced the Conservatives as the official opposition.

Tommy Douglas left his pulpit to contest the Weyburn seat for the party and was defeated. Ten years later (nine of them spent in the House of Commons) he returned to Sas-katchewan to lead his Socialists to a victory that gave the CCF forty-seven seats in the fifty-two seat Legislature and reduced the Liberals to an opposition of five.

The victory at the polls in 1944 had its small beginning at a meeting of angry farmers held in the Town of Indian Head on December 18, 1901. The anger was directed against the rail-roads for their failure to move a bumper wheat crop before winter set in, and as a consequence half the grain was lost.

The protest meeting assailed the railroads, denounced the trade practices of private grain elevators and bitterly spoke out against the monopoly control the elevators exercised over grain marketings. The farmers were seething and mad enough to burn down the elevators and tear up the tracks of the Canadian Pacific Railway's main line which ran past Indian Head.

Farmers addressed the meeting, called for action to form an organization that would protect their rights. Others shouted that it was too late for organization; rather sterner measures were needed, even armed rebellion. Grim-faced grain producers muttered that the only way to stop the fleecing of farmers would be with bullets.

But the peace was preserved and the meeting cooled its anger by getting down to the business of forming the first Saskatchewan farmers' protest movement. It was called the Territorial Grain Growers' Association and its first president was W. R. Motherwell, later a Liberal Minister of Agriculture in the national government.

Emboldened by their status as an organized body, the farmers decided to challenge the power of the C.P.R. in the courts. They brought suit against the railroad, charging that an agent of the company had broken a federal law by showing preference to the elevator companies in the assignment of freight cars. Much to its astonishment and delight, the Association won its case and this strengthened its position in dealing with elevators and grain companies.

The Grain Growers' Association continued to grow in size and influence. Still suspicious of the private elevator companies, it urged the Saskatchewan government to build and operate a system of grain elevators. When the government showed little interest in such a project the Association went to work to develop a number of cooperative elevators which were financed and owned by the membership of the Association. This was the beginning of the Pool elevator system in the Prairies.

When the world price of wheat began to dip, farmers found themselves in a squeeze between falling income and rising costs of transportation and agricultural supplies. The Association charged that big business was robbing the farmer and urged Ottawa to reduce tariffs on manufactured goods.

The federal government was sympathetic but unwilling to tamper with the protective tariffs. Complaining that the old parties were indifferent to the problems of the farmer, the Association began to think about direct political action of its own. Meetings were called to consider the idea of a third political party. The suggestion was put forward that this new party could represent both agriculture and labor. However, the idea ran into opposition and it was shelved for the time being.

With their complaints of economic exploitation by big business and their demands for more government control over transportation and production, the farmers of Saskatchewan sometimes sounded like Socialists. Most of them had never heard of Socialism. Radical as they appeared, and angry as they were against "down east financial interests", the prairie farmers still were going faithfully to the polls to vote for the Conservatives or the Liberals.

A mild form of political Socialism made its appearance in Saskatchewan in 1915. It was an imported type which crossed the border from North Dakota and it called itself the Non-Partisan League. The League worked hard to exploit the discontent of the farmers and convert them to its diluted brand of Socialism. There was no rush to join the League but it did manage to sign up about three thousand farmers before it waned and died as a political force.

The League was unsuccessful in its attempts to arrange a working alliance with the Grain Growers' Association. Leaders of the Association were too closely tied to the Saskatchewan Liberal Party to welcome political interference from an outsider. They persuaded their farm membership that there was nothing to be gained by joining forces with the League.

Agitation for the formation of a new political party was heard whenever problems arose in the farm industry. When crops and prices were good the clamour was stilled. Drought and depressed grain prices followed the end of First World War and the demand for political action flared up again among the farmers.

This time the agitation produced results. On January 6, 1920, determined farmers launched a third political party— the National Progressive Party. This party did the pioneering work that paved the way for the emergence of the CCF. The year the Progressive Party was formed, Tommy Douglas was a school boy in Winnipeg getting ready to start his apprenticeship at the trade of printing.

The rural population rallied behind the new Progressive Party and in the federal election of 1921 the prairie wheat farmers sent thirty-nine Progressive members to Ottawa. Progressives captured fifteen of the sixteen seats in Saskatchewan.

The 1921 election was the new party's best effort. Its political fortunes began to decline after that, largely because much of its support was attracted back to the Liberal camp. Through the decade of the twenties a few Progressives continued to hold seats in Ottawa and in the Saskatchewan Legislature.

When the Progressive Party showed signs of collapsing, a small left-wing group in Parliament led by J. S. Woodsworth, a labour member from Winnipeg who was to become the first national leader of the CCF movement, set to work to preserve the existence of a third party, but one that would espouse a more leftist doctrine than the Progressives.

The left-wing movement put on a drive to see if it could persuade the farmers to support a Socialist party. The proponents of the movement started a program of political education and for the first time in their intermittent history of non-denominational radicalism, Saskatchewan farmers began to learn what Socialism was all about. The farm economy was going through another of its periodic slumps and farmers were in a mood to listen to new ideas and remedies, however extreme.

Left-wingers and labour leaders in Manitoba had formed the Independent Labour Party and now a campaign commenced to form a Saskatchewan branch of this party. The new party was organized about 1930, just as the depression was beginning. J. S. Woodsworth of Winnipeg and M. J. Coldwell of Regina, one of the giants of the CCF movement, worked to weld the new party into a farmer-labour movement.

Perceiving the need for stronger farm support, the leaders of the ILP approached the United Farmers of Canada, the body which had absorbed the Grain Growers' Association, and proposed that the two bodies join forces for political action.

The U.F.C. said it would first wait and see what action Saskatchewan's Conservative government would take on demands made by the U.F.C. for farm relief. When these demands were rejected by the government the farm organization joined forces with the ILP to form a new political movement which would be a Socialist party representing workers and farmers.

The new organization called itself the Farmer-Labour Party and its basic aim was to establish a cooperative commonwealth in Canada. The new movement was taking shape as a national body, too, but calling itself the Cooperative Commonwealth Federation. The Group in Saskatchewan used the Farmer-Labour name until 1935 and then it adopted the CCF label.

The Cooperative Commonwealth Federation was officially inaugurated at a convention in Calgary on August 1, 1932. J. S. Woodsworth was named president of the new party and Norman F. Priestly, vice-president of the United Farmers of Alberta, was the choice for secretary. The party's seven-member provisional committee included some of the pioneers of the Socialist movement: George H. Williams, United Farmers of Canada, Saskatchewan Section; John Queen, labour member of the Manitoba Legislature; William Irvine and Angus Mac-Innis, labour members of Parliament and A. R. Mosher, secretary of the Canadian Brotherhood of Railway Employees and later president of the Canadian Congress of Labour.

The signal to start the offensive against the existing social and economic structure of Canada was given at the party's first national convention held in Regina from July 19 to 21, 1933. This was the convention that formulated the principles of the famous Regina Manifesto—the master plan for turning Canada into a Socialist state. The authors of the document, it was clear, had borrowed ideas and theories from Karl Marx's blueprint for a Socialist order and a classless society.

The objectives of the CCF were candidly set down in the Manifesto. The preamble to the party platform minced no words in stating what the party stood for, where it was going and what it would do when and if it got there:

"We aim to replace the present capitalist system, with its inherent injustice and inhumanity, by a social order from which the domination and exploitation of one class by another will be eliminated, in which economic planning will supersede unregulated private enterprise and competition, and in which genuine democratic self-government, based upon economic equality will be possible. The present order is marked by glaring inequalities of wealth and opportunity, by chaotic waste and instability; and in an age of plenty it condemns the great mass of the people to poverty and insecurity.

"Power has become more and more concentrated into the hands of a small irresponsible minority of financiers and industrialists and to their predatory interest the majority are habitually sacrificed. When private profit is the main stimulus to economic effort, our society oscillates between periods of feverish prosperity in which the main benefits go to speculators and profiteers, and of catastrophic depression, in which the common man's normal state of insecurity and hardship is accentuated. We believe that these evils can be removed

[83]

only in a planned and socialized economy in which our natural resources and the principal means of production and distribution are owned, controlled and operated by the people."

This unequivocal message of intent may have sent a cold shiver or two up and down the spines of Canada's financiers and industrialists. Some of Saskatchewan's destitute farmers were in a frame of mind to give big business something worse than cold shivers. If the Manifesto had promised to put the tumbrils and the guillotine back in service this would have suited the farmers fine.

The CCF's Regina proclamation contained some reassurances for the proletariat. Capitalism was to be eradicated but "the new social order at which we aim is not one in which individuality will be crushed out by a system of regimentation. Nor shall we interfere with cultural rights of racial or religious minorities. What we seek is a proper collective organization of our economic resources such as will make possible a much greater degree of leisure and a much richer individual life for every citizen."

There also was assurance that the CCF would not go about attaining its goals by the Bolshevik method:

"This social and economic transformation can be brought about by political action, through the election of a government inspired by the ideal of a Cooperative Commonwealth and supported by a majority of the people. We do not believe in change by violence. We consider that both the old parties in Canada are the instruments of capitalist interests and cannot serve as agents of social reconstruction, and that whatever the superficial differences between them, they are bound to carry on government in accordance with the dictates of the big business interests who finance them. The CCF aims at political power in order to put an end to this capitalist domination of our political life. . . ."

The devices the CCF would use to rid the economy of Capitalists are outlined in the policy statements of the Manifesto. Planning is the No. 1 plank in the party's fourteen-point platform. Just as soon as they were ensconced in Ottawa the CCF would set up a National Planning Commission whose task it would be to establish a planned, socialized economic order. The Commission would work out a plan for the production, distribution and exchange of all goods and services necessary to the efficient functioning of the economy. It would also co-ordinate the activities of the socialized industries.

The Commission would be responsible to the CCF Cabinet and would work in co-operation with the Managing Boards of the Socialized Industries.

"It is now certain that in every industrial country some form of planning will replace the disintegrating capitalist system. The CCF will provide that in Canada the planning shall be done, not by a small group of capitalist magnates in their own interests, but by public servants acting in the public interest and responsible to the people as a whole."

Socialization of Finance is next on the CCF agenda. The government would take over the administration of banking, currency, credit and insurance. This was necessary in order to have effective control of currency, credit and prices, and the supplying of new productive equipment for "socially desirable purposes."

"Planning by itself will be of little use if the public authority has not the power to carry its plans into effect," said the Manifesto. "Such power will require the control of finance and of all those vital industries and services, which, if they remain in private hands, can be used to thwart or corrupt the will of the public authority. Control of finance is the first step in the control of the whole economy. The chartered banks must be socialized and removed from the control of private profit-seeking interests; and the national banking system thus established must have at its head a Central Bank to control the flow of credit and the general price level, and to regulate foreign exchange operations. A National Investment Board must also be set up, working in co-operation with the socialized banking system to mobilize and direct the unused surpluses of production for socially desired purposes as determined by the Planning Commission . . . insurance companies, which provide one of the main channels for the investment of individual savings and which, under their present competitive organization, charge needlessly high premiums for the social services that they render, must also be socialized."

The party's program of Social Ownership lists transportation, communications and electric power as the first industries that would be brought under government control. Others, such as mining, pulp and paper and the distribution of milk, bread, coal and gasoline, "in which exploitation, waste, or financial malpractices are particularly prominent must next be brought under social ownership and operation."

The Manifesto outlined some of the principles that would apply in placing private industry under social ownership:

"In restoring to the community its natural resources and in taking over industrial enterprises from private into public control we do not propose any policy of outright confiscation. What we desire is the most stable and equitable transition to the Cooperative Commonwealth. It is impossible to decide the policies to be followed in particular cases in an uncertain future, but we must insist upon certain broad principles. The welfare of the community must take supremacy over the claims of private wealth. In times of war, human life has been conscripted. Should economic circumstances call for it, conscription of wealth would be more justifiable. We recognize the need for compensation in the case of individuals and institutions which must receive adequate maintenance during the transitional period before the planned economy becomes fully operative. But a CCF government will not play the role of rescuing bankrupt private concerns for the benefit of promoters and of stock and bond dealers. It will not pile up a deadweight burden

of unremunerative debt which represents claims upon the public treasury of a functionless owner class."

Boards would be appointed by the CCF government to
manage the publicly-owned enterprises: "The machinery of
management may well vary from industry to industry, but the
rigidity of Civil Service rules should be avoided and likewise
the evils of the patronage system as exemplified in so many
departments of the government today. Workers in these public
industries must be free to organize in trade unions and must be
given the right to participate in the management of the industry."

Mindful of the farm support it was recruiting for its political
campaign, the CCF made generous provision for the farmer
in the Regina Manifesto. It promised security of tenure for the
farmer upon his farm on conditions to be laid down by
individual provinces; insurance against unavoidable crop failure; removal of the tariff burden from the operations of agriculture; encouragement of producers' and consumers' co-operatives;
the restoration and maintenance of an equitable relationship
between prices of agricultural products and those of other com-
modities and services; and improvement of the efficiency of
export trade in farm products.

Said the Manifesto: "The intense depression in agriculture
today is a consequence of the general world crisis caused by the
normal workings of the capitalistic system resulting in: (1)
Economic nationalism expressing itself in tariff barriers and other
restrictions of world trade; (2) The decreased purchasing
power of unemployed and under-employed workers and of the
Canadian people in general; (3) The exploitation of both
primary producers and consumers by monopolistic corporations who absorb a great proportion of the selling price of
farm products. (This last is true, for example, of the distribution of milk and dairy products, the packing industry and
milling.)"

The Manifesto promised encouragement and help to co-operative institutions. It said co-operative organizations could be

extended into wholesale distribution and into manufacturing. These enterprises would be assisted by the state through appropriate legislation and through the provision of adequate credit facilities.

In the section dealing with Taxation and Public Finance the CCF promised that in place of taxes upon articles of general consumption "we propose a drastic extension of income, corporation and inheritance taxes, steeply graduated according to ability to pay. . . ."

"An inevitable effect of the capitalist system is the debt creating character of public financing. All public debts have enormously increased, and the fixed interest charges paid thereon now amount to the largest single item of so-called uncontrollable public expenditures. The CCF proposes that in the future no public financing shall be permitted which facilitates the perpetuation of the parasitic interest-receiving class; that capital shall be provided through the medium of the National Investment Board and free from perpetual interest charges."

The program of the CCF proposed that all public works, as directed by the Planning Commission, be financed by the issuance of credit based upon the national wealth of Canada.

The Manifesto had something to say about Freedom. The CCF would guarantee freedom of speech and assembly for all; it would repeal Section 98 of the Criminal Code (this section was designed to suppress Communist activity during the Thirties; it was subsequently repealed by a Liberal government); the CCF would amend the Immigration Act to prevent "the present inhuman policy of deportation"; the party promised equal treatment before the law of all residents of Canada irrespective of race, nationality or religious or political beliefs.

The Manifesto adds this further comment to its policy on freedom:

"In recent years, Canada has seen an alarming growth of Fascist tendencies among all governmental authorities. The

W. Ross Thatcher, M.L.A.

most elementary rights of freedom of speech and assembly have been arbitrarily denied to workers and to all whose political and social views do not meet with the approval of those in power. The lawless and brutal conduct of the police in certain centres in preventing public meetings and in dealing with political prisoners must cease. Section 98 of the Criminal Code which has been used as a weapon of political oppression by a panic-stricken capitalist government, must be wiped off the statute book and those who have been imprisoned under it must be released. An end must be put to the inhuman practice of deporting immigrants who were brought to this country by immigration propaganda and now, through no fault of their own, find themselves victims of an executive department against whom there is no appeal to the courts of the land. We stand for full economic, political and religious liberty for all."

For labour, the CCF program supported a National Labour Code which would give the worker maximum income and leisure, insurance covering illness, accident, old age and unemployment, freedom of association and effective participation in the management of his industry or profession. The party promised to implement a system of socialized health services. It termed the Canadian Senate "a standing obstacle to progressive legislation" and this body was marked for abolition along with Capitalism.

The final paragraph of the Regina Manifesto reiterates the warning that a day of judgment awaits the capitalists when the people finally see the light and send a CCF government to Ottawa:

"No CCF Government will rest content until it has eradicated capitalism and put into operation the full program of socialized planning which will lead to the establishment in Canada of the Cooperative Commonwealth."

This was the declaration of policy and principle enunciated by the new Socialist party at its first national convention in

Regina in July, 1933. Afire with the righteousness of their cause, delegates hurried back to their homes across Canada to begin the work of paving the way for Socialist governments to take over in the provinces and in Ottawa.

Almost thirty years after the adoption of the Regina Manifesto only one of the delegates to that convention had seen his work pay off in a mandate from the electors of one province to carry out some of the provisions of the Manifesto. Mr. Douglas of Weyburn successfully exploited the depression and the discontent of farmers to bring the CCF to power in Saskatchewan.

The temper of the farm population made it responsive to the radical reforms temptingly proffered by the Socialists. With their festering grievances against big business, the farmers saw in the Regina Manifesto an instrument of retribution and retaliation. In normal times, with crops and prices good, the traditionally conservative farmer might well have rejected a programme which posed a threat to the freedom and independence he prizes so highly. But in the Thirties, with their fields parched and their granaries empty, the economic theories of Socialism looked good to desperate men.

Not all the farmers were quite that desperate. There were some who quickly ended their connection with the party after they had read the content of the Regina Manifesto. This document of intentions left them uneasy and apprehensive. They found something alien and ominous in the form of government it would seek to impose on Canada. Repelling, too, was the idea of an all-powerful hierarchy of bureaucrats, boards and commissions controlling the economic life of the nation.

Many farmers were alarmed and angry when the more left wing elements in the party attempted to make nationalization of land a plank in the CCF platform. The proponents of this principle argued that it would protect the farmer against dispossession by mortgage and investment companies and guarantee him permanent land tenure. Farmers replied that they would rather take their chances with the mortgage companies than become mere employees of the state. The party dropped the idea.

The farm vote elects governments in Saskatchewan and the CCF had this very much in mind when they were drafting the party's programme for agriculture. Farm security figured prominently in the programme. The CCF promised to introduce legislation to provide protection and security for farmers on their land. During the 1944 election campaign CCF candidates quoted figures on foreclosures and evictions and declared that "the farms of Saskatchewan are passing into the hands of mortgage and loan companies."

Campaigner Douglas promised security of land ownership for the farmer. Douglas said that farm evictions would cease under the CCF. He declared that a CCF government would resign if a single farmer was evicted from his land.

Mr. Douglas was reminded of this promise to resign by Liberal Leader Ross Thatcher during the 1961 session of the Legislature. Thatcher, quoting from official records, pointed out that between 1945 and 1959 there had been 1,931 farm foreclosures, 354 evictions and 1,066 cancellations of agreements for sale. Douglas did resign a few months later but farm evictions had nothing to do with it.

The victory of the CCF was an electoral rebuke to the old parties by a rural population protesting nine years of drought, dust and destitution. The end of the dry cycle and the outbreak of Second World War once more gave the farmers wheat to sell at good prices but the conditions of the Dirty Thirties were not forgotten when the farmers went to the polls in 1944.

The CCF in its bid for power under the leadership of Tommy Douglas wrung every nickel's worth of political advantage out of the depression. For a young, new party it conducted a shrewd, aggressive campaign and it was contending against a formidable Liberal organization which could draw upon the experience of thirty-four years in office. But the depression was on the side of the CCF and the result was a landslide for the Socialists.

It was a tremendous personal victory for Mr. Douglas. He had staked his political future on the outcome and he had given the campaign everything he had. The victory was the sweeter for the fact that he had beaten one of the biggest men in the business of winning elections—the Hon. James G. Gardiner, federal Liberal Minister of Agriculture, who had used his prestige and political know-how to help the provincial Liberal effort.

The Socialist triumph in Saskatchewan sent tremors through the whole free enterprise structure of Canadian business life. It rocked the old parties, too. Socialism had established a bridgehead in the Prairies. The statistics of the election underscored the strength of this bridgehead. The Douglas forces had taken forty-seven of the fifty-two seats in the Legislature. And the party's share of the popular vote was an impressive fifty-three per cent.

Premier Douglas briskly applied himself to the task of choosing the personnel of his cabinet. He was anxious to get on with the job of putting into practice the ideas and theories of government that had been laid down in the 1933 Regina Manifesto.

The Premier's ministerial appointments set up a cabinet composed of men with solid party backgrounds. These were the appointees to the first cabinet of the Douglas administration:

T. C. Douglas—premier and minister of health.

C. M. Fines, a Regina school principal — provincial treasurer.

J. W. Corman, K.C—attorney-general.

G. H. Williams, a farmer—minister of agriculture.

J. H. Brockelbank, a teacher and farmer—minister of municipal affairs.

O. W. Valleau, a farmer—provincial secretary and minister of social welfare.

J. J. Phelps, a farmer—minister of natural resources.

J. T. Douglas, a farmer—minister of highways and public works.

Woodrow S. Lloyd, a school principal—minister of education.

J. H. Sturdy, a school principal—minister of rehabilitation and reconstruction.

L. F. McIntosh, a cooperative field agent—minister of cooperatives.

C. C. Williams, a railroad telegrapher and a former mayor of Regina—minister of labour.

This was the composition of North America's first Socialist government. Three only of the original cabinet still remain in office. Death, election defeat and retirement removed the others. Mr. Douglas left the government in the fall of 1961 when he accepted the leadership of the New Democratic Party.

He gave up the office of premier at a time when the winds of change were blowing in the province. Discontent was stirring again in the rural areas. Farmers were facing some of the same old economic problems of the Thirties and they were bleakly unresponsive when Mr. Douglas' successor, the Hon. Woodrow S. Lloyd, in a radio address to the province, called for a spirit of "togetherness" and put forward the novel proposition that citizens should consider it an honour and a privilege to pay taxes.

6

Debate at Mossbank

Mossbank, SASKATCHEWAN, is a small, quiet farming community fifty miles southwest of the City of Moose Jaw. The most exciting event in the village's slow-paced history occurred on the wet, cold spring night of May 20, 1957.

Canadians across the nation were celebrating Victoria Day.

The Village of Mossbank wore a festive air despite the rain but the crowds that poured into the village during the afternoon and early evening had come to witness fireworks of a kind not usually associated with the annual celebration of Queen Victoria's birthday.

The event was a public debate and it would bring to the platform in Mossbank's little community hall two men who had been friends before a political defection involved them in one of the bitterest personal feuds in Canadian political history.

With an animosity and a flow of invective seldom heard in public life, Premier Douglas of Saskatchewan threw out a challenge to ex-CCFer-turned-Liberal Ross Thatcher to meet him on a public platform. Thatcher agreed to face the debating skill of the formidable Douglas and the meeting was set for May 20 in Mossbank.

The acceptance of Douglas' challenge by Thatcher made news across the country and reporters from big eastern papers arrived in Mossbank to cover the story. They anticipated that it would be the story of Thatcher's crushing defeat under the slashing tongue of Douglas.

Cavalacades of cars bearing jubilant CCFers arrived in Mossbank with horns blaring. The Douglas supporters were confident their man would murder the CCF defector and they were looking forward to an evening of rare sport. Liberals supporting Thatcher were glumly certain, too, that this would be the fate of their man. Mossbank's normal population of six hundred swelled to three thousand that night but those with money to wager on the outcome could find no takers. Nobody was interested in risking money on Ross Thatcher.

This was the mood of the crowds in Mossbank that rainy Victoria Day as they waited for the hour to arrive when the debaters would face each other on the platform.

The debate that was to take place in the community hall in Mossbank was the climactic point in a political drama which had its beginning in the House of Commons when Ross Thatcher, CCF member for Moose Jaw-Lake Centre, rose to his feet one day and committed heresy. While his CCF colleagues gripped their seats and listened in shocked amazement Thatcher told the government it was going too far with its welfare measures and then to make matters worse he declared that corporation taxes were too high.

Party Leader M. J. Coldwell dressed him down for talking like a Capitalist. But Thatcher was not to be subdued. He continued to disagree with the social and economic policies of his party and in April, 1955, ten years after he entered Parliament as a CCF member, he left the party but remained in the House as an independent.

As an independent he brought down upon his head the sizzling anger of Tommy Douglas when in May, 1956, speaking in the Pipeline Debate, he spent some time reviewing the financial record of Saskatchewan's Crown Corporations and he called it a record of waste, failure and incompetence.

[95]

Two months later, in July 1956, Mr. Thatcher crossed to the government side of the House and took his place as a Liberal. The Calgary Herald said he looked more natural sitting over there:

"Colorful and well-liked as he was, Mr. Thatcher just never looked right sitting in the CCF ranks anyway. He was an anachronism, a wealthy young Capitalist merchant sitting among lean, hungry and non-Capitalist Socialists."

Under CCF attack from the day he quit the party, Thatcher invited trouble in earnest when he decided to contest the riding of Assiniboia for the Liberals in the 1957 federal election. This was the seat held for the CCF since 1945 by Hazen Argue—Thatcher's roommate in Ottawa before he left the party.

If they had been unkind in their remarks about the defector before, Douglas and Argue now opened up on him with no holds barred. The pair of angry politicians were further provoked when Thatcher in campaign speeches disclosed that one of his reasons for leaving the CCF was because extreme left-wingers were making inroads into the party organization.

Argue heaped scorn on his former friend for his political defection: "I would not call him a second-hand candidate. He has become a third-hand political candidate."

If Mr. Argue had had the gift of foresight he would have kept his mouth shut. Five years in the future Hazen Argue was to reach a point of no return in his political career and make his lonely decision in the home and in the company of Ross Thatcher. Then he would cross the floor to the Liberal camp and become a second-hand politician.

And Argue's reasons for leaving the New Democratic Party would echo the same disillusionment and disenchantment that Thatcher gave for his defection. The man who was going to want badly the leadership of the New Democratic Party and lose it to Tommy Douglas, would make the accusation that the NDP was financed and dominated by a clique of big leaders . . .

"class control of a national political party now acquired within the NDP constitutes a dark and sinister threat to democratic government in Canada."

And as an epilogue to his indictment of labour's domination of NDP affairs, Argue would first praise the CCF Party and then bury it. This eulogy and this funeral service would constitute Hazen Argue's farewell to his political past and his rejection of principles and beliefs he could no longer subscribe to:

"The CCF has made a contribution to political development in Canada, far in excess of its numerical size. The CCF has championed with courage and vigor many public issues in the common good . . . the CCF as we have known it, has now ceased to exist . . . Socialism as a viable political force is dead and this is as it should be . . . the Regina Manifesto has proven to be impractical, out of step with reality and at variance with Canadian traditions."

And faced with this defection of another old friend and political colleague, Douglas, in February, 1962, would declare that Argue's expressed reason for leaving the New Democratic Party "is nothing more than a smoke screen to cover up his abject betrayal of his friends and his political party.

"Mr. Argue saw no labour bogeymen in the NDP organization and administration until he was beaten by me in the leadership contest."

It was said of Douglas that he inspired fierce loyalty from his colleagues and party workers. But this loyalty seemed to be subjected to some strain after Mr. Douglas took the CCF into the NDP fold. Some of his previously devoted adherents appeared to feel that Douglas in a sense had defected, too. At the time Hazen Argue quit the party there was evidence of growing discontent and insurgence in CCF circles. Reports were rife that two minor members of the Saskatchewan cabinet were willing and ready to fly the coop with a little encouragement from Ross Thatcher's Liberals.

The Liberals, however, were not showing too much enthusiasm. "We took Argue," said a Liberal MLA, "but we have to draw the line somewhere."

But the parting of political ways between Tommy Douglas and Hazen Argue was still five years away in the future when Douglas was stumping the constituency of Assiniboia in 1957 to win support for "my friend, Hazen" and defeat that "liar and traitor" Ross Thatcher.

Thatcher's House of Commons attack on the Crown Corporations filled Douglas with a blazing, implacable anger and he vowed to settle accounts with the former CCFer. Douglas was further provoked when the Financial Post published Thatcher's version of the Crown Corporations' financial histories. Douglas asked the Financial Post for the same amount of space to present the government side of the picture and the paper's editors agreed but only on the condition that they first be allowed to conduct an independent audit of the Corporations' financial affairs. Mr. Douglas indignantly rejected this condition and for about a year no Saskatchewan government advertising appeared in the Post.

The 1957 federal election campaign in the riding of Assiniboia developed into a bitter and acrimonious contest. Douglas stalked Thatcher from platform to platform and labelled the new Liberal a renegade for his criticism of the Crown Corporations. And Thatcher fanned the flames of Douglas' wrath by repeating over and over again that the government's experiments in industry had been a fiasco and a failure.

Douglas charged that Thatcher had chosen the riding of Assiniboia to seek re-election because he was afraid to go back and face the people of Moose Jaw-Lake Centre who had elected him to Parliament as a CCF member.

"I say he's afraid to go back and meet these people for he would be tarred and feathered in some parts of the constituency, and he knows it," Premier Douglas asserted.

Thatcher had a rough voyage during the campaign. He received anonymous letters containing threats to slash the tires of his car and pelt him with rotten eggs. CCF hecklers harassed his meetings and rumors circulated that plans were afoot to "rough him up" at one meeting place or another. At one stage of the campaign it was reported that Thatcher was trying to recruit a bodyguard of wrestlers but he denied this. As it turned out, the Liberal candidate came through the campaign unharmed.

A far cry now from his Weyburn pulpit, Douglas unmercifully lashed his opponent and thundered that he was going to "drive Ross Thatcher out of the province." Douglas was addressing a meeting in the town of Ogema when he challenged Thatcher to meet him for a debate on a public platform.

"He may as well make up his mind to have a joint meeting because I shall hound him from one end of the constituency to the other," the Premier declared.

The day after Douglas issued the challenge the newspapers reported that Thatcher would accept. The Liberal said that the language used by Mr. Douglas in calling him a liar and traitor was strange for a provincial premier, and he regretted that Mr. Douglas had taken such an attitude.

"I also find it strange that he should wait five months to comment on the speech I made in the House of Commons on Saskatchewan Crown Corporations," said Mr. Thatcher. "He claims that I spoke in Parliament where people could not know whether my statements were true, and where they could not be answered. Surely he cannot object to an MP speaking in that chamber. Ten CCF members at Ottawa had every chance to refute my figures if they so desired. Does he feel that they were not capable of looking after CCF party interests?

"Moreover, I may say that I made the same speech in Moose Jaw during the last provincial election, which was duly reported, yet neither the premier nor any of his ministers challenged it to my knowledge. I have no wish, or desire, to distort any figures—as far as I know my sources of information were correct."

Mr. Thatcher said he welcomed the opportunity to debate the subject with the premier on an appropriate occasion in the future. Thatcher said that since he had been challenged he should have the right to choose the time and place.

Douglas didn't agree with this: "I am not aware of any rule which prescribes that the one challenged has the privilege of choosing the time, place and conditions of the debate. In all previous experiences I have had in matters of this sort, the debate was held under joint sponsorship and arrangements were made by mutual agreement."

But Thatcher would not concede this and Douglas reluctantly gave in. The Liberal chose Mossbank as the place for the debate and proposed that Dr. F. H. Wigmore, a Moose Jaw Progressive-Conservative, officiate as the neutral chairman. Douglas agreed to these terms.

They had some trouble reaching agreement on a date for the debate. Dates Thatcher suggested were not agreeable to Douglas; dates Douglas proposed were not satisfactory to Thatcher. These negotiations had been carried on by correspondence and it was not until the two accidently met on a street in Weyburn that the date was firmly fixed: May 20.

Following agreement on the date, Mr. Douglas had some second thoughts about Mossbank's suitability as the place for the debate. It occurred to the Premier that the big rink in the City of Weyburn would be a better place. He accordingly dispatched a letter to Thatcher suggesting this change:

Dear Mr. Thatcher:-

Ever since the public announcement of the proposed debate on May 20th a great many representations have been made to me to the effect that the community hall at Mossbank cannot possibly accommodate the larger number of people who would like to attend.

I believe it would be possible to secure the rink at Weyburn where 5,000 people could easily be accommodated. It may be that there are other centres in the constituency which would accommodate a large crowd and which you would prefer as a location for the meeting in question. However, I would like you to consider Weyburn as a possible meeting place.

I shall of course agree to holding the debate in Mossbank if you are insistent that this is the one point in the constituency which is acceptable to you.

Yours sincerely,

T. C. Douglas.

Thatcher was insistent. The idea of holding the meeting in Douglas' home constituency in front of a crowd which not by chance would be predominantly pro-Douglas in its sympathies did not appeal to the Liberal at all. Mossbank, said Mr. Thatcher firmly.

The Commonwealth, official organ of the Saskatchewan CCF Party, sneered at Thatcher's refusal to meet Douglas in Weyburn. Said the paper in its edition of May 15, 1957:

"If Ross Thatcher had a just case to present to the public in his debate with Premier Douglas, he would want to have as many people as possible on hand in the biggest hall or rink available. But his insistence upon holding the debate in Mossbank community hall indicates clearly that he wants as few witnesses as possible to his political eclipse."

It was an eclipse CCF supporters at Mossbank confidently expected to see and Liberals feared would happen. Ross Thatcher awaited the contest with some foreboding, too.

The debate captured the imagination of the province and had it not been for the rain the crowd in Mossbank that night might have numbered ten thousand instead of three thousand.

CCF and Liberal supporters brought picnic baskets with them but the weeping skies ruled out supper on the grass. The Liberals took their baskets to the community hall and the CCF dined in their cars in the grounds of the village school. Sensing an easy victory, the CCF crowd relieved its high spirits by driving around the community hall with horns blaring to annoy the more subdued Liberals inside.

Hours before the starting time of the debate the crowds were lined up in front of the door of the community hall. Nine hundred squeezed into the hall itself and another two hundred settled down in the basement to hear the proceedings over loudspeakers. Two thousand sat outside in their cars in the dripping night to listen to loudspeakers or catch it on their radios.

The stage was finally set for the great debate and the hour had arrived. Radio microphones, television cameras and lamps were in position. Premier Douglas and Ross Thatcher occupied chairs in their respective corners. Chairman Wigmore was ready to give the signal for the curtain to go up.

Dr. Wigmore announced the rules:

"The first speaker, the Premier of Saskatchewan, will open the debate and have forty minutes to present his case . . .the second speaker, the Liberal candidate for Assiniboia, will be given forty minutes to present his case . . . and a further ten minutes during which time he may make his rebuttal . . . the first speaker will then close the debate in a ten minute period."

The audience could applaud but it mustn't heckle, the chairman warned.

The debators stood up and shook hands. Thatcher took his seat again and Douglas advanced to the lectern to set about the task of annihilating the Liberal. CCF supporters gave Mr. Douglas a thundering ovation.

Premier T. C. Douglas: Mr. Chairman, Mr. Thatcher, Ladies and Gentlemen.

I want to welcome you all to this debate here in Moss-bank tonight. Mr Thatcher and I just shook hands before we came on the platform. I don't want anyone to misinterpret that gesture. We shook hands for the same reason as the fellow who was holding hands with his wife. His friend said to him—"You and your wife have been married for 30 years, what are you holding hands for?" and he said—"If I don't hold hands with her, she is liable to sock me one".

I want it clearly understood at the beginning, that this debate is being confined to Saskatchewan's Crown Corporations at the insistence of my opponent tonight. I notice the Regina Leader-Post has a cartoon suggesting that we ought to widen the terms of this debate to general federal issues. I would like to say right here and now that if Mr. Thatcher will say the word, I am prepared to throw this speech away and to discuss federal issues and to prove, I think, to the satisfaction of this audience, that the Liberal government, and particularly Mr. Howe and Mr. Gardiner, have brought western agriculture to the verge of bankruptcy.

I heard some booing. I think that is some of the sheep that Jimmy Gardiner paid $100,000 for. Well, the booing seems to continue. I have a stop-watch here and if it continues . . .

Spectator: Crown Corporations, Mac!

Spectator: Shudup!

Mr. Chairman: I will brook no interruptions from the floor.

Mr. Douglas: Now, I know this audience will give to Mr. Thatcher and myself a courteous hearing. I want to say that the reason for this debate is, that last year on the 22nd of May, in the course of the Pipeline Debate, Mr. Thatcher made a very strong attack on the Saskatchewan Crown Corporations. He made statements which, in my opinion, were misleading, and incorrect and, consequently, I asked him to substantiate those statements in a public debate.

I did so, not because I object to anyone criticizing the Crown Corporations. They are public enterprises and the business of public affairs is to discuss and to criticize public affairs. What I did object to, was a member from Saskatchewan, standing up in the House of Commons and making statements which misrepresented and maligned his province.

I have just come back from a series of meetings in Ontario. I find that at every meeting, Liberal candidates are quoting the speech which Mr. Thatcher made and saying . . .

Mr. Chairman: I must inform the speaker that he must not refer to the other speaker by name.

Mr. Douglas: I have known no rule of this procedure, Mr. Chairman. These rules were never read to me prior to this debate, but I will refer to him as the Liberal candidate, if that suits you better, Mr. Chairman.

Mr. Chairman: That is according to the rules, Sir.

Mr. Douglas: And, I find that Liberal candidates across the country are quoting this speech, telling people that all the Crown Corporations in Saskatchewan have folded up, that they have been a dismal failure, and they say the best proof of it is that these statements were made by a man who lives in Saskatchewan and who is a former CCF member of parliament.

However, I want to deal with that speech and I want to ask Mr. Thatcher—or my opponent—when he is speaking, to either substantiate the statements which he made in the House of Commons or admit that he was misrepresenting the situation as far as these Crown Corporations are concerned.

Now, I can't quote all of his speech. That would take all of my 40 minutes. But, after all, you don't have to drink a whole pot of soup to know what the soup is like. All you need is to have a few spoonfuls, and I am going to take some of the illustrations which were used by the Liberal candidate, when he spoke in the House of Commons. I will start with what he said about the Saskatchewan Housing Corporation. He said that it had a deficit of $42,400. Now, I have here the financial statement from which he must have been quoting —it is the only financial statement issued to the members of the legislature, to the Crown Corporation Committee. It has five columns, the 'total net deficit', 'total net surpluses', 'adjustments', 'net deficits' and 'net surpluses'.

What does the Housing Corporation show? Housing Corporation shows, total net deficit, $42,400; adjustment $133,-100; net surplus $90,700. What is the explanation for that? When we set up the Housing Corporation, we did so after the war to prepare to provide housing accommodation for veterans and their families. We provided some 445 suites; we provided housing accommodation and board for some 305 veterans and their families who were attending university. We did so, under an agreement with the Central Mortgage and Housing Corporation by which they were to pay a certain amount in lieu of the contribution which would normally be coming from the federal government. We knew that money would come. It took some time in coming but nevertheless, it was part of the agreement. Therefore, we knew that this $150,000 was coming and so there isn't a deficit of $42,000, there is a surplus of $90,000. Why did my opponent quote the first column in the financial statement and not the second column?

Now, my opponent is not an inexperienced boy. He is a university graduate in economics; he was for many years a high executive for Canada Packers; he has been a successful businessman; and for 12 years a member of the House of Commons. He knows what a financial report means and here in the House of Commons, he says, that this Crown Corporation had a deficit of $42,000 when actually it had a surplus of $90,000. Moreover, he said that it closed up in 1947 with the impression, of course, that it went broke. It didn't close up. These houses are still being operated for veterans but they were turned over to the Department of Social Welfare, since the actual task of converting them into suites had been finished and it was a matter of continuing to operate.

This is the interesting thing. When this member was speaking about these buildings being turned into homes, he made no reference to the fact that the Saskatchewan Reconstruction Corporation, in turning war buildings and war assets into cash had shown a return to the people of Saskatchewan of $395,000. When he was mentioning housing, why did he not mention the Reconstruction Corporation?

We'll take another example. My opponent referred to the

Fish Marketing Service. He has spent much time castigating the Fish Marketing Board. Then he turned to the Fish Market-ing Service and said "although it has only been operating a few years, it has an accumulated deficit of $180,000." Now, this same financial statement which I have here in my hand, shows that it had that year a surplus—an operating surplus of $30,417. Now, the only way I can account for this gentleman talking about an accumulated deficit of $180,000, is that he has taken into consideration the payments which were made by the Department of Natural Resources for floor prices for fishing.

Now, I know that he doesn't believe in floor prices. In the House of Commons, he opposed the floor price of 58 cents a pound for butter and I have the Hansard here for anyone who wants to see it. He may not believe in floor prices, but the CCF government does believe in floor prices and over a period of years, we have paid out in floor prices to fishermen $222,000 as at the end of 1955. We have aver-aged about $32,000 per year. Some years we didn't pay any-thing, other years we paid more, but the average was about $32,000 a year. We think that money was well spent. That kept hundreds of fishermen from having to go on social aid; and enabled them to earn a decent living and gave them a guaranteed price for their catch.

Now, my opponent may not agree with floor prices, and that is his privilege. But the fact that he doesn't agree with floor prices doesn't give him the right to take floor price pay-ments made by the Department of Natural Resources and add it on to the operating expenses of the Marketing Board and call that a deficit, when actually there was an operating surplus of $30,417.

And, to take another example. He made reference to the Brick Plant at Estevan. He said that the government sank $900,000 in this venture and had a deficit of $176,000. Now, as a matter of fact, those figures are not quite right. The capital investment is $750,000. There was a writeoff on the old plant of $102,000, making a total of $852,000, but my opponent took the $102,000 writeoff and he added it to the capitalization, and then he also added it to the accumulated deficit. Now, you can't count a writeoff twice. If he does that with his income tax he is going to get into trouble some day. You can't do that! So that at the time he was speaking, if you add the writeoff to the capitalization, there was a capitalization of $852,000 and there was a deficit at the end of 1955 of $73,448 and the surplus for 1956 wiped out. The Brick Plant is now operating in the black.

Why didn't he tell the House of Commons all the facts? That this plant was started by a private company; that it closed in the '30s; that it operated for only brief periods for nearly 15 years; that the government reopened it. Of course, we had difficulties with the operation, because the equipment was old and obsolete. When we put in tunnel kilns it immediately began to show good results.

Why didn't he tell the House of Commons, for instance, if he were proud of Saskatchewan, that in 1953 the Brick Plant showed a surplus of $39,642 or 5.3 per cent return on the capital investment; that in 1954 it showed a surplus of $36,672 or 4.9 per cent return on the capital investment; that in 1955 it showed a surplus of $56,986 or 7.6 per cent return on the investment; and last year it had a surplus of over $70,000 and that plant is now operating in the black.

The Premier warmed to his task. He was on familiar ground. This route he had travelled before, defending his Crown Corporations. With the righteous and assured air of a man dealing in unassailable facts, Mr. Douglas' nimble tongue went on reeling off impressive columns of figures to demonstate that Ross Thatcher's bookkeeping was for the birds. The Douglas school of arithmetic ousted Thatcher's deficits and replaced them with surpluses.

Mr. Douglas denied Thatcher's charge that private operators of sodium sulphate plants had been forced to sell out to the government. The government had acquired one plant from an owner who was in financial difficulties.

"Now we have a plant at Chaplin and a plant at Bishopric and why didn't my friend, when he was making his speech about Crown Corporations, tell the House of Commons that in 1955 these sodium sulphate plants had accumulated profits of $659,000 and that they paid royalities of $287,000, making a total of $946,000. As a matter of fact, at the end of 1956, these two sodium sulphate plants have paid in surpluses and royalties, $1,157,000 on a capital investment of only $1,085,-000," said Mr. Douglas.

The government bus company was another example of Thatcher's carelessness with facts and figures, the Premier noted sorrowfully. Far from the meagre profits the Liberal computed, the bus company at the end of 1956 was showing an accumulated surplus of $432,000.

It was not true either, said Douglas, that the Government Insurance Office secured its business by compulsion.

"Every dollar that is paid for insurance under the Automobile Insurance Act goes into the Automobile Insurance Fund. Not one dollar goes from that fund into the Saskatchewan Government Office. The only time that money goes out of that fund, it goes out to pay benefits to people who are injured or dependents of those who are killed. The Saskatchewan Government Insurance Office doesn't get a five cent piece from the insurance on your car or truck which you buy when you buy your license. Sure, if you buy a package policy that is different, but on the compulsory insurance, the insurance office doesn't get a nickel. Why doesn't my opponent make a statement like that in the House of Commons where people can carry a story like this back to their communities?"

Mr. Douglas did concede that institutions receiving grants from the government were compelled to buy their insurance from the government insurance office. This compulsion applied to hospitals, sanitaria, schools, orphanages and other institutions.

However, said the Premier, this business in 1955 represented less than 4½ per cent of insurance written by the government office.

At the end of 1955, Douglas reported, the government insurance office had an accumulated surplus of $2,291,000.

The fact that three Crown Corporations—the shoe factory, the tannery and the woollen mill—lost money and closed up was nothing to get disturbed over, said the Premier. He was reminded of something President Roosevelt used to say:

"You must trust us by out batting average. Sometimes we hit a home run, sometimes we strike out."

The batting average was pretty good, the Premier considered. The Corporations to the end of 1955 had returned a net surplus of $6,372,000.

"The people of the province invested in these Crown Corporations up to the end of 1955, $9,634,000, and in that year they had a return of 14.18 per cent on the capital investment. In addition, the Corporation paid to the government royalties of $946,000."

And having completed the job of converting Thatcher's deficits to surpluses, Mr. Douglas closed his ledgers and moved on to another area of grievance. As well as seeing red in the financial affairs of the Crown Corporations, Ross Thatcher had found a bright tinge of Red in the CCF itself.

Said Mr. Douglas with some heat: "My opponent has been going around this constituency, particularly in places which are not covered by the press, and he has been saying that he knows things about people inside the CCF and that he has photostatic copies of private files from the R.C.M.P. which show that there is a CCF MLA who has associations with the Communists."

The chairman interrupted the Premier to suggest that perhaps he was straying from the point.

"I am saying here, Mr. Chairman, that instead of discussing this in some private corner of the constituency, I am inviting the Liberal candidate to put this photostatic copy of a confidential file of the R.C.M.P on this table. I am inviting him to tell me how he came in possession of a confidential file of the R.C.M.P. I want him to tell me whether or not he has the file with the knowledge and consent of Mr. Garson, the Minister of Justice, and to tell me whether or not Liberal candidates are being given confidential files from the police in order to carry on election campaigns."

While the village hall rocked to the roar of hoots, hollers, cheers and applause, Mr. Douglas ended his forty-minute address and returned to his seat in the corner.

It was now the turn of Ross Thatcher, the underdog. The din broke loose again and the chairman banged his gavel to quiet the crowd. But it was curiosity rather than the gavel that silenced the nine hundred spectators. How now would Thatcher acquit himself after taking that verbal pommelling from Tommy Douglas?

"The Liberal candidate for Assiniboia will now present his case and he will confine his remarks to the Crown Corporations of Saskatchewan," directed the chairman. "No interruptions from the floor please."

Mr. W. Ross Thatcher: Mr. Chairman, Mr. Premier, Ladies and Gentlemen.

First of all, I would like to say that it is a pleasure for me to be here tonight in the village of Mossbank, particularly for the purpose of debating Saskatchewan's Crown Corporations.

I felt a moment ago that perhaps the Premier was a little bitter. I can't say that I blame him for not talking about Crown Corporations at all for the last 10 minutes of his speech because the record is pretty bad. The Premier said that my speech has done great disservice to my province in the east. I believe it has done great disservice to the CCF party and I hope that that is true.

Now, Mr. Chairman, how did this debate come about? In May, 1956, as the Premier told you, I made a speech in the House of Commons pertaining to the record of Saskatchewan's Crown Corporations. Five months later, the Premier, at the Assiniboia CCF Nominating Convention, took violent exception to my remarks.

Well now, in the first place, he charged that I lacked courage to make those statements in Saskatchewan where I could be answered. Very respectfully, I will tell the Premier that I have made those speeches on many platforms in Saskatchewan, but even if this were not so, I fail to see how the Premier can object to a Member of Parliament speaking on any subject in the House of Commons. When I made that speech, to which my opponent objects, CCF federal members, including I believe my opponent in the Assiniboia constituency, were there. They had every opportunity, in debate, to refute either the statements made or the figures used.

Now, according to newspaper reports of that Assiniboia CCF Nominating Convention, the Premier challenged me to debate the subject on any public platform. He said in effect: "He may as well make up his mind to have a joint meeting, because I shall hound him from one end of the constituency to the other". Well, Mr. Chairman, I know that the Premier is a busy man and I wouldn't want him spending all his time down in this constituency, although he has been spending a good deal. Therefore, I am happy to accept his challenge.

Well, Mr. Chairman, the original Crown Corporation program was launched shortly after the CCF came to power in 1944. Prior to that date Socialist speakers constantly deprecated the fact that private enterprise had not established industry in Saskatchewan and they deplored the fact and, rightly I think, that thousands of young citizens in Saskatchewan in those days, were forced to go down to the United States or to B.C. or down east to find employment. One of the CCF planks which appealed to me most, as a young man, was the promise to end this situation.

Now the Premier and all Socialists from the Premier down,

said: "If private capital would not establish industry in Saskatchewan, we shall do it ourselves by state ownership and thus provide employment". And at the same time the Premier and CCF spokesmen promised the people extensive, free, social services and these services were to be financed in considerable part from the profits of the government-owned industries. I quote the Regina Leader-Post of June 13, 1944, the Premier said this: "The CCF proposes to get money for its social service program by the government engaging in revenue producing businesses."

Now, these then I say respectfully, Mr. Chairman, were the original objectives of this experiment in state Socialism. I frankly admit that no one supported that program more enthusiastically than I. That is, until I learned the true facts.

Since taking office, the Socialist government has either set up or taken over 19 Crown Corporations. And in those companies, as nearly as I can ascertain at the present time, they have invested approximately $175 million of the taxpayers' money. After 12 years of experimentation, I suggest that three questions should be posed and considered by the people of Saskatchewan tonight.

First of all, have the Crown Corporations been able to operate efficiently?

Secondly, has the government, because of the program, been able to provide a substantial number of additional jobs for Saskatchewan citizens in manufacturing industries?

Thirdly, have the Crown Corporations made revenue available to the provincial treasury which it could use for social services, highways, school grants, etc.?

I believe that the answer to these three questions will tell us whether state Socialism in Saskatchewan has succeeded or failed.

Well now, let us look for a moment at some of the individual companies. One of the first enterprises set up was the leather tannery. What are the facts pertaining to that company? The purpose of the leather tannery was to tan cow-hides and make them into leather. 1946 was a year of short supplies and high prices, the best possible condition under which to commence operating an industry. And yet the activities of the tannery were ill-fated and short-lived. About the only hides they tanned were the hides of the Saskatchewan taxpayers.

And so the company moved from one economic crisis to another until December, 1948, when the employees were thrown out of work just before Christmas. And when all the smoke had cleared away, that company had a deficit, as nearly as I can ascertain, of roughly $200,000. One company up, one company down!

A shoe factory was set up in 1945 to utilize the leather which was made in the tannery. What are the facts pertaining to the shoe factory? I recall Premier Douglas speaking at Brandon, Manitoba, and he announced and I quote from his speech: "The tannery and shoe factory now being operated by the CCF can make shoes for $2.75 a pair". Well, in spite of the Premier's optimism on that occasion, the shoe factory did lose money, so much so that in 1948, it closed down after having accumulated deficits of more than $82,000. Two companies up, two companies down!

A woollen mill was set up in my home city of Moose Jaw. What are the facts pertaining to this operation? The paper theory behind this operation was reasonable, but the industry was in difficulties from its opening day. When it was finally forced to close in 1951, it had accumulated deficits of $830,-000 and it paid none of the interest of $206,000 on its advances. The mill was transferred to a private company. That company finally moved the machinery out of the province and today the whole operation is defunct. Three companies up, three companies down!

And now I come to the Housing Corporation. The Hous-ing Corporation was set up after the war to convert military huts into housing accommodation that could be rented. And it should be noted that the CCF government, which has been so noisy in its demands for the federal government to build low rent housing, has done virtually nothing in this field itself. We have one of those housing projects in the City of Moose Jaw up near the Exhibition Grounds. And I have seen better housing condemned for slum clearance.

And yet despite the fact that CCF progress in building housing was extremely limited, in a relatively short period of time, the Corporation was able to accumulate deficits of $42,-000. Now, the Premier said tonight my figures are wrong. "Why", he said, "there should have been a government grant in that figure from the federal government." Well, I have a question in my hand which was asked of Mr. Fines on February 21, 1956. That question was this: "What audited statement or report shows an accumulated surplus of $90,699 for the Saskatchewan Reconstruction Housing Corporation? Answer: No audited statement or report shows an accumulated surplus of $90,699 for the Saskatchewan Reconstruction Housing Corporation."

Now, the government, as it time and again does, takes a federal grant or a provincial grant and suddenly puts it in the revenue account of a Crown Corporation and then turns around and says that actually it has been making money. That Housing Corporation in 1947 was closed down despite what the Premier says. That is four companies up and four companies down!

Very early in its first term of office, the CCF government set up a Fish Board, and they built a number of fish filleting plants in northern Saskatchewan. Every commercial fisherman in a defined area was compelled to sell his fish to the Board. Despite that fact, almost from its inception the Corporation lost money and I think that the situation was all the worse because it frequently paid the fishermen less than they could have obtained from private buyers. After accumulating a deficit of roughly $400,000 which as usual did not contain interest on advances, the government closed down in 1949. Five companies up, five companies down!

The Fish Board then was replaced by the Fish Marketing Service. From the start the government concealed the losses of this new Board by making an annual grant, and at the end of the last fiscal year, the Premier told us that they were showing a surplus of $32,000. In fact, I say that that figure is little more than fiction because to arrive at this amount, provincial grants of $242,000 are included as revenue.

In 1951, the lumber mill was set up at Big Beaver, Saskatchewan. Within a year and a half the mill reported a deficit of more than $97,000 and it cost the treasury another $54,000 in interest on advances. Well, having thus demon- strated itself as subject to heavy deficits, in 1953 it was merged with the Timber Board. Since then its results have been concealed under the surpluses or behind the surpluses of the Timber Board.

The box factory at Prince Albert was expropriated from a private corporation under pretty drastic legislation. The man- ager of the plant, when it was under private ownership, was ordered by some of the government Socialist planners to follow a certain course of action. He refused on the grounds that such a policy would bankrupt him. The Socialists then moved in and confiscated the plant. Since that day the box factory has been in financial difficulty. During the last year alone, according to the government's own figures, it had a loss of $133,000, bringing its accumulated deficits to the rather shocking total of $352,000. That whole operation has been a fiasco, and should be sold back to a private company which knows the economic facts of life.

The surprise of the evening was Mr. Thatcher. Upsetting all predictions, the Liberal showed no signs that he had been squelched or intimidated by the Douglas eloquence. His voice was strong and his arguments cogent. He spoke like a man who had done his homework carefully and he stuck to the topic of the debate—the Crown Corporations. Prudently he ignored the attempts of his opponent to entice him into other dangerous areas of controversy.

But the story of the Crown Corporations Mr. Thatcher unfolded was quite unlike the one that had just come from the lips of Tommy Douglas. The deficits were back where the surpluses had been. The audience could have sworn it was hearing about two different sets of Crown Corporations.

Thatcher made some changes in the Premier's financial statement on the government brick plant. The capital investment in this industry amounted to $750,000, said the Liberal. But despite the fact that the plant was operating during a nation-wide construction boom and enjoyed a virtual monopoly supplying brick to government building projects, its history had been one of technical problems, selling difficulties, over-production and high employee layoffs.

"According to the government's own figures up to March, 1956," said Mr. Thatcher, "the company had a deficit of $105,000. The Premier tells us tonight that this has now been wiped out, but if interest on advances is included, and why shouldn't it be, the true picture shows the deficit would be very substantial even today."

It was true that some of the Corporations had shown substantial profits, the Liberal admitted. But almost without exception these were business operations which thrived under government compulsion, some form of monopoly or government privilege.

"The Saskatchewan Government Printing Company is a good example," said Thatcher. "Over the years it has accumulated net profits of slightly more than $500,000. Why shouldn't it? The printing company is supplied by the government with all the work it can do—profitable printing at non-competitive prices."

The Timber Board? This was another profit-maker, said Thatcher. Up to the end of 1956 it had accumulated surpluses of $3,500,000. How did it do this?

"The Socialist government gave the Timber Board an almost complete monopoly of lumber harvested in Saskatchewan. Producers are compelled by law to sell their timber to this Board at relatively low prices. Then the Board goes out into the high markets of Canada and the United States and resells the lumber. The company does provide employment for many people. Yet it is also a fact that its operations have resulted in the closing down of many private sawmills and associated businesses."

The Fur Marketing Board? This enterprise had shown operating surpluses during the period trappers were required by law to sell their beaver and muskrat skins through the Board, said Thatcher. But when this state monopoly was discontinued at the insistence of the trappers, the profits of the Board dropped sharply.

"Now I come to the Saskatchewan Government Insurance Office," said Mr. Thatcher. "The office has had a substantial financial growth as the Premier has pointed out. Speaking on the provincial radio network, Mr. Kuziak (the Minister of Natural Resources) claimed that the company was commenced in 1945 with a government investment of $12,000. 'Today', he boasted, 'it has assets of over $12,000,000.' That is half a truth. Mr. Kuziak deliberately neglected to mention that the company also had liabilities of $9,600,000. The insurance company, since its inception in 1945, has accumulated a surplus of $2,340,000. At first glance this surplus is very gratifying. I want tonight to apologize to the Premier for saying that the auto insurance went into this fund. That was my original belief. I was in error, Sir, and I want to apologize for it."

The Liberal then went on to point out that a good deal of the business done by the insurance company was obtained by compulsion. In addition to the institutions mentioned by the Premier, said Thatcher, government buildings formerly considered fireproof were required to take out insurance with the government office.

"The Premier claims that the Government Insurance Office forced all other companies to reduce rates in Saskatchewan, and at one time I think that was the case, but today the opposite is frequently true. Both board and non-board companies are frequently underselling the government company. Repeatedly, these private companies are forcing the Government Insurance Office to reduce rates in order to compete. As a result of private competition last year, the Government Insurance Company had an underwriting loss of $132,000. The Saskatchewan Guarantee & Fidelity Company was purchased by the government in 1949 at a cost of $250,000, and this company, since its inception, has accumulated surpluses, but once again a considerable portion of the business has been obtained by compulsory methods. For example, owners of commercial trucks and public service vehicles are compelled by law to purchase various kinds of insurance and guarantee bonds from this company. Electrical contractors, gas contractors, electrical supply houses, are likewise ordered to buy guarantee bonds from this company. On the type of business where it has to compete, the company has steadily run into increasing difficulties. So much so that in the last fiscal year the Saskatchewan Guarantee & Fidelity Company had a net loss of $103,000."

The bus company? According to Mr. Thatcher's figures the bus operation, despite the monopoly it enjoyed, had shown only nominal profits, six-tenths of one per cent on its investment in 1955, and 3.5 per cent in 1956. And, the Liberal pointed out, had it paid interest on its advances it actually would have lost substantial sums of money.

"The Saskatchewan Transportation Company was set up after the CCF took over," said Thatcher. "It took upon itself a monopoly of those bus routes which were not interprovincial by their nature. A number of private operators had their lines arbitrarily expropriated. For example, we have one man in this audience tonight who had his bus business confiscated by the government. He is Mr. H. B. Legge of Moose Jaw who had operated a busline from Moose Jaw to Riverhurst for seven years. Overnight he was put out of business to make way for the government company. Now the ironic feature of the Legge case is the fact that the government after operating the line for a short period of time and finding it unprofitable, abandoned it. CCF speakers claim that the Saskatchewan Transportation Company provides service to areas where private enterprise won't go. Well, the Moose Jaw-Riverhurst line would indicate that in some instances citizens were deprived of a service they previously enjoyed under private enterprise."

From buses Liberal Thatcher moved to electric power and natural gas. He was not impressed by the Premier's boast that the Saskatchewan Power Corporation had put into effect five different power rate reductions since 1949. Thatcher produced figures to show that even with these reductions power rates in Saskatchewan were about seventy per cent higher than comparable rates in Manitoba.

"Now, let us look at the field of gas," said Mr. Thatcher. "The Power Corporation, of course, has set up a gas monopoly. The Premier has made this statement on numerous occasions and I think he made it tonight: 'The great advantage of public utilities is that they operate on a service at cost basis.' Well, as far as gas is concerned, I say that this is quite an admission for the Premier to make because it certainly follows that Power Corporation gas costs are far out of line when compared to Alberta companies, whether private or public."

Gas consumers in the City of Moose Jaw, the Liberal said, were paying twice as much for the fuel as the people of Calgary and two and a half times as much as consumers in Medicine Hat.

And having swept through the Crown Corporations like a Texas Tornado, Mr. Thatcher cast an eye over the wreckage and then proceeded to challenge the Premier's statement that the companies had made 14.18 per cent on their investment.

"In order to arrive at that figure he has indulged in a

fantastic example of arithmetical gymnastics," said the Liberal. "According to the Crown Corporation auditors themselves, the companies last year made, not 14.18 per cent, but 3.7 per cent. And if all expenses had been properly charged, they would have made 3.4 per cent."

The Premier, said Mr. Thatcher, had come up with a surplus of $6,372,000, but in the process he had overlooked a few debits which should have been applied against this figure: $2,289,000 in interest on investment; $498,000 in grants; $565,000 as the cost of operating the Government Finance Office; $307,000 for the government's purchase of defunct corporations; $449,000 for auditing expenses.

When these charges were taken into account, said Thatcher, the Premier's reported surplus of $6,372,000 melted down to $2,264,000.

The Liberal candidate seemed prepared to go on with the melting process, but time was running out. Ending his scrutiny of financial performance, Mr. Thatcher turned to the question of what the Crown Corporations had done to provide better employment opportunities in manufacturing.

"And I remind you that since the war, manufacturing capacity in Canada has tripled. Thousands of new plants have been built, thousands of plants have been extended, hundreds of thousands of new workers have been employed," said Thatcher.

What about manufacturing in Saskatchewan?

"On April 17, Mr. Chairman, I wrote the Dominion Bureau of Statistics and I asked them a very simple question: How many people were engaged in Saskatchewan in manufacturing industries in 1945; how many are engaged in manufacturing in 1956? And, Mr. Chairman, I shall table these figures for your perusal as soon as I finish speaking. They are indeed shocking, because they show that despite the spending of $175,000,000 by the CCF government in Crown Corporations, despite the fact that manufacturing everywhere else in Canada has doubled and tripled, we have at the end of last year, 67 fewer people in manufacturing than in the first year of the CCF in office. In other words, I say that these Corporations have failed in their second major objective and I challenge the Premier to show where that is not so in his rebuttal."

Another objective of the Crown Corporation program was to provide money for social services, highways, education and health. How well had they succeeded in this regard? Mr. Thatcher's answer was that the companies had not contributed a single five cent piece to highways, education and the other services.

"As a matter of fact, ladies and gentlemen, quite the contrary is true. Millions have been drained off by this Socialist government, spent in costly Socialist experiments—money which otherwise would have been available for better old age pensions, better highways, better grants to education and municipalities."

His audit completed, Mr. Thatcher sat down. His Liberal supporters sat up and cheered. Their man had taken the measure of the champion and a legend of invincibility had been punctured. The CCF bloc booed but the boos lacked conviction. Thatcher's performance had dampened the spirits of the pro-Douglas multitude.

Now it was Mr. Douglas' turn again. But the Premier was to find that in the ten minutes at his disposal he would not be able to do much to repair the damage that Thatcher had done in fifty minutes of steady, concentrated demolition work.

"The meeting will come to order please," said the Chairman. "The Premier of Saskatchewan has now ten minutes for rebuttal and I ask you to give him your attention."

Mr. Douglas answered Thatcher's charges that power and gas rates in Saskatchewan were too high:

"For instance he talked about power being cheaper in Manitoba than it is in Saskatchewan. Of course it is. In Manitoba they had a government that started to put in rural power thirty years ago. We had a Liberal government in Saskatchewan that did nothing about putting in power. We put in power when materials were costing four and five times what it cost in Manitoba, plus the fact, of course, that we had to travel many miles to supply the same number of customers as they do in Manitoba. He compared gas rates. He was very careful to compare gas rates with Medicine Hat, Calgary, and Edmonton who put in their gas systems thirty years ago when steel cost a fifth of the cost per ton that it is today. Those firms have already paid off their entire capital investment and today are charging only operating costs plus a good profit."

Douglas compared gas rates in Saskatchewan and Manitoba. He found that citizens of Winnipeg were paying up to 34 cents more for 1,000 cubic feet of gas than the citizens of Regina or Moose Jaw.

Mr. Douglas had a ready explanation for the fact that the number of employees in manufacturing in Saskatchewan seemed to have shrunk since 1944. The figures quoted by Mr. Thatcher came from the Dominion Bureau of Statistics which obtained them from the federal Department of Labour which counted employees only in plants over a certain size. Consequently, said the Premier, these figures would not include employees in smaller factories in the province.

Besides, these statistics covered only employment in manufacturing, the Premier pointed out. Jobs in all types of industry in Saskatchewan had increased by 10,000 since 1944.

The Premier disputed Thatcher's statement that not a five cent piece had ever gone from the Crown Corporation's into the provincial treasury:

"As a matter of fact," said Mr. Douglas, "the Crown Corporations have not only paid money into the provincial treasury but every dollar in addition has been plowed back into the extension of services. A surplus of $34,000,000 at the end of 1956, has been plowed back into providing more power, more services, more gas, for the people of the province. And I want to say this, that I believe the people of this province recognize that the Crown Corporations have made a genuine contribution to the economic life of this province and no amount of misrepresentation and maligning of these Crown Corporations by my opponent of the Liberal Party is going to divert the people of Saskatchewan from going on with the task of building the kind of Co-operative Commonwealth that my opponent started out to build but then lost heart and fell by the wayside."

The great debate was over. It may not have settled conclusively the financial status of Saskatchewan's Crown Corporations and it may not have shed too much light into the more clouded corners of the Corporation accounting system, but it did establish that Ross Thatcher was a much better debater than anyone had realized. He had battled it out toe-to-toe with the Terrible Tommy and for years to come mention of the Mossbank debate would go on precipitating arguments over the question of who won it.

A Calgary Herald reporter covering the debate, had this to say of the result;

"Ross Thatcher emerged from the now famous Mossbank debate as a new power in Saskatchewan politics—not because he won but because he did not lose.

"When Thatcher agreed to meet Premier T. C. Douglas at the Village of Mossbank and debate the now threadbare Saskatchewan issue of whether or not Crown Corporations have been a success, few expected him to emerge with his hide intact.

"That he did, has been a moral victory for the anti-CCF groups and some dismay to the CCFers."

The Liberal Regina Leader-Post, predictably, had words of praise for Thatcher's part in the debate:

" . . . Mr. Thatcher succeeded in doing what others have tried to do without success, prick the balloon of the Saskatchewan CCF leader's invincibility in debate. Mr. Douglas at last has found his match, not in invective, nor in rapier thrusts, nor in demolishing personal attacks, but in a presentation the effectiveness of which lay in sheer weight of its material and its sound logic."

Douglas had his own answer for those who said Thatcher had bested him: "We'll know who won the debate on June 10 (federal election day)."

Whether or not the debate had anything to do with it, Thatcher lost the election in Assiniboia to his CCF opponent Hazen Argue. But far from going into political eclipse as the CCF Party organ, The Commonwealth, had predicted would be the Liberal's fate after the Mossbank debate, Ross Thatcher went on to win the leadership of the Liberal Party in Saskat-chewan. And in the not too distant future the chances are good that Thatcher will occupy the big office on the second floor of the Legislative Building where Douglas held sway for the seventeen years he was Premier.

Crown Corporation profits reported by the government come under fire every year in the Saskatchewan Legislature. The 1962 session was no exception. In language reminiscent of the Mossbank debate, Liberal financial critic A. H. McDonald disputed a government claim that the Corporations up to 1961 had made profits totalling $12,250,000.

The report of these profits, said Mr. McDonald, was not an audited statement and presented a false picture of the actual situation. The Liberal listed four items of expense which he said were charges against the Corporations but which were not included in the report. Mr. McDonald did some subtracting and when he was through the Corporations' profits of $12,250,000 had shrunk to $1,200,000. The Liberal also pointed out that no deductions had been made for grants, auditing costs, printing charges and the purchase price of assets of defunct Corporations. Take these away from what was left of the profit, said McDonald, and there would be no profit left. Mr. Thatcher had arrived at the same conclusion in Mossbank in 1957.

7

Climate For Industry

THE PROVINCE that hitched its hopes to
the Douglas star in 1944 has had seventeen years to reflect
on that decision and to wonder if Saskatchewan would have
fared better under another form of government.

One criterion of government performance is economic
development: production, jobs, payrolls. Industrial development
in Saskatchewan under Socialism is good by the standards of
comparison the CCF employ. The Socialists compare the
present with the past. They point to the industrial status of the
province as it was in 1944, a year when the economy was
just beginning to flex its muscles again after a decade of depression and economic stagnation.

But measured by the industrial growth and diversification
that have taken place in the other three western provinces
since 1944, Saskatchewan's record is not good. With possibly
the exception of Prince Edward Island and Newfoundland,
Saskatchewan lags behind the other Canadian provinces in
manufacturing development and jobs in manufacturing.

In his debate with Mr. Douglas at Mossbank in 1957,
Ross Thatcher contended that in the year 1956 the factories of
the province employed 67 fewer people compared with the
number employed the year the CCF took office. The Premier's
answer to this charge did nothing to disprove it. Douglas
argued that Thatcher's figures covered only employment in

manufacturing whereas when all industrial jobs were taken in account the result showed an increase of 10,000 jobs over the 1944 figure.

Mr. Douglas did not go on to say where all these new jobs were. Oil development and uranium mining would account for many of them. But even as Mr. Douglas was debating this question with Ross Thatcher, many of these 10,000 new jobs were disappearing. The oil play had reached its peak and was waning. The market for uranium was shrinking and some of the big northern mines would soon be forced to close down —mines which at peak production provided employment for almost 2500 men.

Twenty-seven thousand urban unemployed in the province in 1961 tragically underlines the inability of the Douglas administration to obtain for Saskatchewan an equitable share of the new factories built in the Prairies since 1944. The value of manufacturing in Alberta between 1950 and 1960 rose from a figure of $400 million to a level of $900 million; in the same period manufacturing in Manitoba climbed from $486 million to $738 million; Saskatchewan's manufacturing production in this decade increased from $218 million to $330 million.

Manufacturing plants in the Province of Alberta numbered 1800 in the year 1960; Manitoba had a total of 1716 factories; Saskatchewan's figure was 1083. In 1961, Saskatchewan's neighbor to the west employed 34,000 in manufacturing; Manitoba provided 39,000 factory jobs; Saskatchewan's employment in manufacturing totalled 10,000.

Desperate as the province's need is for industrial expansion, its methods of attracting industry have been called ineffectual and inept. Bemused businessmen who have had dealings with the government's agencies claim that the experience had the flavor of Alice's Adventures in Wonderland.

This bemusement is not confined to outsiders. A Saskatchewan civil servant, his cynicism brimming, affixed to the top of his desk with scotch tape a little printed card which read: "You don't have to be crazy to work here, but it helps."

And having executed his small sedition, this disenchanted public servant removed himself from the government payroll. He joined a quite considerable company of disillusioned ex-employees of what the government brightly refers to as its Industrial Development Office.

Business people and a large segment of the general public —CCF supporters included—today subscribe to the view that somewhere in the mechanism of the government's industrial development apparatus a screw is loose.

The loose screw, in part at least, is perhaps the condition of schizophrenia which afflicts Saskatchewan's Socialist government in its attitude to competitive business. It is a difficult trick to inveigle private industry into the province whilst at the same time proceeding with plans to establish a new social order in which there is little or no place for Capitalism. Free Enterprise can hardly be blamed for showing some reluctance to accept an invitation which somehow or other was uncomfortably remindful of an invitation by the hangman to step into the death cell!

The credits and debits of the Socialist experiment in Saskatchewan to date have produced a balance sheet from which is missing the rich dividends that were promised the electorate in 1944. The Douglas formula for abundant living was all neatly built around the largesse that would flow from the profitable operations of a complex of government enterprises. This was the cure for unemployment and the means to banish depressions for ever. This was the system that would pay the bill for CCF social services. Free Enterprise had failed miserably to do the job. And who needed Free Enterprise anyway? This was Mr. Douglas talking in 1944.

The Douglas plan for economic self-determination was neat, unique and exciting. There was only one fault with it: It didn't work. And when the experiment collapsed, the Douglas government suddenly discovered that it needed Free Enterprise after all. Wheat, tax revenue and federal subsidies alone are not sufficient to keep an economy vigorous and robust and the CCF administration in a quick change of political pace and policy dusted off the welcome mat, shaped its scowl into a fair imitation of a salesman's smile and invited private capital to come in and build some factories.

As further proof of its kindly intentions toward private business, the Douglas government set up an industrial develop-ment office and established an industrial development fund. The job of the office was to lure industry to the province and the purpose of the fund was to sweeten the lure with offers of industrial loans.

Well-intentioned as these services may have been, the gov-ernment could not resist the temptation to bring them under Socialist influence and turn them to propaganda use. These new branches of government might have been effective if administ-ered by experienced, non-political businessmen. But the Social-ists like to give these jobs to friends who will not overlook the extra-curricular political chores that go with the jobs. The government placed in charge of the new services two of its thoroughly indoctrinated followers, men who had been schooled in the principle of public ownership and steeped in the gospel of the Regina Manifesto.

While its efforts to attract industry have not been very suc-cessful, Saskatchewan's Industrial Development Office has measured up as a classic example of the bureaucratic bumbling and boondoggling described in Parkinson's Law. Critics of the office accuse it of ignoring its real function in its preoccupation with ways and means of spending public funds in order to qualify for larger operating budgets.

Concerned at the lack of industrial growth in Saskatchewan and distrustful of the methods the government was employ-ing to attract industry, Colin McConechy, executive editor of the Moose Jaw Times-Herald, set out to examine the situation and ask businessmen across the province what they thought about the government's attempts to encourage industry.

Mr. McConechy put down his finding in a series of articles written in 1961 for his paper. Since the Industrial Office (set up by Premier Douglas and his responsibility as minister in charge) functioned as the principal agency entrusted with the task of promoting industry, McConechy focussed his attention on the job this office was doing. He found evidence to support the view that the job was not being done well:

"Periodically there has been great drum beating as the Industrial Development Office publicizes a conference called by the Industrial Development Office to tell civic officials or businessmen or newspaper people how industry is developed.

"Those so summoned assemble, listen politely, display the proper enthusiasm, comment, generally on the value of an industrial development office, then they return home. That will be all until the Industrial Development Office again calls them together to hear the word."

McConechy suggested that after ten years of "something less than lacklustre development" a more realistic procedure would be for the businessmen and civic officials to call the next conference and seek an accounting from the Industrial Development Office.

"The shoe would be put on the proper foot. The Industrial Development Office is employed by these tax-paying businessmen and civic officers. They have been picking up their share of the $180,000-a-year tab to have the office develop industry."

The Moose Jaw newspaperman posed the question: Are they getting their money's worth? Is the office operating efficiently in the best interests of the province as a whole? Does its work compare favorably with the accomplishments of similar organizations in neighboring provinces?

McConechy said the answers to the questions could be found in any of the major centres of Saskatchewan:

"The opinion that the Industrial Development Office is not, and has not, been doing the job it should and could for Saskatchewan is expressed in strong terms throughout the province. Over several months, I've heard it in Regina, Saskatoon, Prince Albert and Moose Jaw.

"In the latter three cities the view expressed is that the industrial office has contributed little or nothing to the development of these centres. Such opinion, unfortunately, is expressed always on a 'don't-quote-me-by-name' basis. While informed, the sources are reluctant to allow their names to be published. They maintain the government through its many inspectors and purchasing agents could make things rough for them in a business way.

"Saskatchewan is low man on the industrial development totem pole in the three prairie provinces. And that's about as polite a presentation of the province's plight as is possible," said the newsman. "The value of new industry in Alberta this year (1961) must nearly double that of industry established in Saskatchewan in the last five years. Manitoba is getting new industry at the rate of three or five for every one coming to Saskatchewan.'

It was the feeling of those he spoke to, McConechy said, that not all the blame for Saskatchewan's poor showing industrially could be laid at the door of the Industrial Development Office:

"Many insist the greatest deterrent to development is the fact this province has now the only Socialist government in power in the Western World. The threat it poses of interference in the business life of the province bears the bulk of blame for Saskatchewan's failure to keep pace with its neighbors."

The Douglas government does not make a practice of publicly admitting error in what it does.

Privately, Mr. Douglas was willing to concede that the industrial office was a pretty sad affair. But this private view notwithstanding and just a few months after expressing it,

Douglas upped the man in charge of the office to the rank of deputy minister. Promotion in the CCF can be dictated by considerations other than merit.

It was on the occasion of this promotion that the Premier took the opportunity to rid himself of the rather embarrassing portfolio of minister of industry. The job was passed on to a junior colleague, the Hon. Russ Brown, who had served his apprenticeship as a political organizer for the party before winning a seat in the Legislature and then a Cabinet post.

Saskatchewan's Industrial Office may not have brought many factories to the province but it is entitled to some recognition for the ingenuity and imagination it displays in making much out of little. Saskatchewan is probably the only province in Canada to come up with the novel idea of fattening up a lean report on new industries with the addition of a church, a senior citizens' home and a skating rink.

The office has staged some memorable press conferences. One of the biggest and most elaborate of these affairs was convened in 1958 to announce a $60 million pulp mill for the province. Preparations for the conference were conducted in strict secrecy. Provincial Treasurer C. M. Fines headed a committee of four whose task it was to mount guard over the surprise until Mr. Douglas could take the wrappings off at the designated hour and exhibit his prize to the press corps.

Unfortunately one of the members of the committee was a frequenter of two political camps and the night before the press conference this custodian of the secret unwisely joined a group of Liberals making merry at a party. The Liberals plied him with strong liquor and out popped the story of the pulp mill. The morning papers carried it some hours in advance of the time set for the press conference.

There was consternation and cries of foul play but the conference went on and the surprise that was no longer a surprise was unveiled with proper ceremony. Mr. Robert Campbell of Vancouver, the man who was to put up the

$60 million to build the pulp mill, apparently felt that the conference should not be deprived of its surprise. And as special surprise, Mr. Campbell casually broke the news that he would toss in another $10 million for a potash development.

The announcement of the pulp mill and the potash mine made some large headlines in the provincial press. This was nice for Mr. Douglas with an election just a few weeks away. The CCF won the election with the help of some enthusiastic voters who made their homes in areas of the province that had been indicated as probable sites for the mill and the mine.

The mine and the mill unfortunately never materialized. Three or four pulp mills have been coming to Saskatchewan since the CCF took office but none has ever quite managed to make it. The Liberal opposition in the Legislature unkindly draw attention to the fact that these pulp mill announcements always seem to crop up just before an election. The Hon. Russ Brown, minister of Industry and Information, announced in March, 1961, that new interest was developing in the province's pulp potential. This inevitably aroused the speculation that an early provincial election might be in the offing.

Saskatchewan has been a happy-hunting ground for industrial promotors from Vancouver. Two very shrewd operators named J. W. Sharp and Jack Turvey appeared in the province about 1956 and thoughtfully appraised the great gaps in the province's industrial structure. The two industrial prospectors entered into negotiations with the government. The outcome was Saskatchewan's first cement mill, built with financial assistance from the government and on the understanding that the government would support home industry by purchasing its cement from the mill. A year or two later the mill was profitably sold to Inland Cement Company.

Casting about for another likely vein of ore to tap, Messrs. Sharp and Turvey this time saw the possibilities of a plant to produce steel transmission pipe for the oil and gas industries. They approached the government with this proposal and the government bought it; sanctioned another loan and promised that the natural gas division of the Saskatchewan Power Corporation would buy its pipe from the new industry.

The plant was built and it prospered. The government was happy with the success of the new industry, the power corporation was happy with the pipe it bought, and Turvey and Sharp were not unhappy with the profits they were pocketing as a reward for their initiative and enterprise.

Their appetites whetted for new conquests, the Turvey-Sharp team again reconnoitered the industrial landscape and this time produced for the government's inspection an idea that was big, bold and expensive. It was a proposal for a basic steel mill. Mr. Douglas and his advisors took a little more time to digest this one but they were finally persuaded that steel production would jolt Saskatchewan out of its industrial lethargy and tone up the whole economy. And with another election coming up, a steel mill was as good as if not better than a pulp mill.

The government agreed to advance money and furnish guarantees. The mill was estimated to cost about $16 million. In a return asked for by the Liberal opposition during the 1961 session of the Legislature, the government disclosed that it had guaranteed loans to the steel mill totalling $14,500,000. There was also the disclosure that it had made a loan of $610,000 to a firm called Industrial Consultants Limited. This firm it transpired was another operation of Turvey and Sharp. And leafing through the prospectus of the steel mill the Liberals noted with interest that the mill was obligated to make payment of $237,000 to Industrial Consultants Limited for supervisory services.

The government had a field day with the announcement of the steel industry. Mr. Douglas termed it the most important development in Saskatchewan's industrial growth. He predicted that the mill would make Saskatchewan "the Pittsburgh of the Prairies". There was further fanfare and ceremony when the sod was turned at the plant site north of Regina in the fall of 1958. The Premier wielded the gold spade. Then the work of construction began. By the spring of 1960 the building was up and most of the mill equipment had been installed. Press, civic officials and other dignitaries were on hand to watch Provincial Treasurer C. M. Fines pour the first ingot.

Everything was rosy up to the end of 1960. The newspapers faithfully carried the bright progress reports issued by President Sharp and Secretary-Treasurer Turvey. Mr. Douglas was still talking about his "Pittsburgh of the Prairies". The Industrial Development Office had adopted Mr. Sharp as its patron saint. The local Chamber of Commerce was sponsoring his nomination for the title of Canada's Man of the Year.

January of 1961 signalled the start of steel production at the mill and it was also the signal for trouble. The steel the mill produced was defective. For many months thereafter the industry was plagued by production, sales and money problems. A succession of experts was called in to try and solve the technical difficulties. Behind the scenes government, directors and management wrestled with the industry's financial problems and the press hinted at stormy sessions.

There was a report that Mr. Douglas was urging the management to find a buyer for the mill. The board of directors took a look at the salaries paid the executive staff and the company cars they were driving and suggested some changes might be in order. Hundreds of shareholders entranced by the Douglas vision of a "Pittsburgh of the Prairies" bought in at $5.40 and watched the vision slowly evaporate to a market value of $1.50. The shareholders were not made happier by a disclosure in a newspaper that friends and relatives of government cabinet ministers were on Mr. Sharp's executive payroll.

The newspaper reported that the former head of the government finance office—the office which processed government loans to the steel mill—had been installed as assistant to company president Sharp; the post of office manager had been assigned to the son of Clarence Fines, provincial treasurer at the time the steel mill received government loans; traffic officer for the company was the title given to the son-in-law of the Hon. Russ Brown, the minister of Industry and Information.

As was to be expected, the Liberals pounced on this juicy situation with the enthusiasm of kids scrambling for free candy. They criticized the government for risking so much public money in such a precarious venture. Liberal Leader Ross Thatcher suggested it was not at all unlikely the province would wind up with another unprofitable Crown Corporation on its hands. Liberals asked for an investigation into the affairs of Inter-provincial Steel & Pipe Corporation.

Doing some poking into the business of the company themselves, the Liberals noted that a feature of the promotion of the steel mill was the sale of 310,000 shares at 60 cents a share and the sale of 705,153 shares at $5.40 a share.

Of the 60 cent shares, 180,000 were sold the Saskatchewan government as consideration for the government guaranteeing a first loan of $10 million. Directors of the company were permitted to purchase 60,600 of the 60-cent shares along with 176,273 at $5.40 a share.

One item in the company prospectus that stirred the Liberals' curiosity and left it unsatisfied was the statement respecting the disposition of the remaining 69,400 shares in the 60-cent bracket. These shares, the prospectus stated, "are presently held by 49 private individuals who are or have been employees of the company or of other companies in which some of the directors have interests or who are persons whom it was felt were in a position to contribute to the welfare of the company by way of substantial personal investment, acquisition of markets and other similar reasons."

Prospects were brighter for Saskatchewan's steel industry in the spring of 1962. Technical problems had been overcome, steel produced was meeting required standards and sales were better. The progress reports coming out of the mill had regained something of their old aplomb. The company, however, let it be known that it would still be interested in talking to prospective buyers. Mr. Sharp and Mr. Turvey, in the spring of 1962, were still directing the affairs of the mill but somewhere along the way they had discarded the idea of becoming the architects of Saskatchewan's industrial revolution.

Mr. Douglas some months before this had carefully considered the troubles at the steel mill and his "Pittsburgh of the Prairies" was quietly down-graded as a dream.

The Liberals, unimpressed by the reports of improved conditions at the mill, were still repeating their demands at the 1962 sitting of the Legislature for an investigation and they were still being ignored by the government. Suspicious that the government had made new loans to the company, Mr. Thatcher asked the government to table the names of companies and the loans they had received during the past fiscal year. The government refused on the grounds that it would not be in the interest of industrial development.

Industrial development in Saskatchewan has provoked some hot debates in the provincial Legislature. The Douglas administration was sensitive on this point and the opposition made the most of it. One of the most punishing attacks on the CCF's industrial record was made by the leader of the opposition during the Legislative session in February 1961. Mr. Thatcher devoted most of an hour-long speech to criticism of economic development under Socialism.

The Liberal leader, a former CCF member of Parliament, opened his address by conceding that all political parties generally were seeking the same goals and objectives: a better province, new industries, full employment and a better deal for the farmers.

"We differ, then," said Mr. Thatcher, "not as to our main goals and objectives, but rather as to the best methods which should be used to achieve these objectives. The CCF propose

to build a better Saskatchewan by travelling the Socialist road
—the road of government ownership. Here, we Liberals differ
fundamentally. We believe that private initiative and individual
enterprise can accomplish much more for our people than
Socialism."

That said, the Liberal settled down to some good old-fash-
ioned rough-and-tumble speechmaking. One of the reasons
for unemployment in the province, he charged, was the failure
of the Socialists to persuade new industries to locate in Saskatchewan.

"In view of that failure," said Mr. Thatcher, "I was amazed
at the colossal gall of the government in the Throne Speech
to state that 'industrial growth in Saskatchewan continues to
maintain an encouraging pace'. Who finds Saskatchewan's industrial growth encouraging? That is one of the most ridiculous
statements ever heard made in this House."

The Liberal leader said Mr. Douglas was being a bit devious
and tricky when he claimed that new investment in Saskatchewan for the year 1960 was estimated at $600 million and
that this indicated "the faith investors have in the great future
of Saskatchewan."

Mr. Thatcher said the Premier left the impression that this
was the figure which business and industry invested in the
province during the year.

Investment in ordinary industry was only a part of it,
said the Liberal. The figure also included a large sum invested
by farmers in farm machinery and repairs. It included capital
expenditures on roads, hospitals, schools and other services by
provincial, municipal and private authorities. It included expenditures on houses, apartment buildings, churches and stores.

"In other words," said Mr. Thatcher, "when you boil it all
down, industry in 1960 invested not $600 million in Saskat-
chewan, but actually only about $23 million in manufacturing.
The real figures indicate anything but confidence on the part of
investors in Saskatchewan, under a Socialist government.

The Liberal leader fixed a critical eye on 32 new industries announced by the government and proceeded to boil them down, too.

A foundry at Lumsden, he declared, employed two people; a lawn ornament factory at Saskatoon employed the owner and his wife; a septic tank and monument firm at Wynward provided work for five people; a soap factory at Regina would employ up to eight people and a Saskatoon company manufacturing television tubes expected to use five workers.

"These five industries," said Mr. Thatcher, "are typical of the ones that the Throne Speech claims 'are evidence of the diversification that is taking place in Saskatchewan industry.' I ask the House to note that the total employees of the five plants I have mentioned will be 21. Many of the remaining 32 companies mentioned by the government fall into the same minor category."

The Liberal next turned his attention to what he called the government's "make-believe" industries.

"About 2600 years ago a famous Greek was born," said Mr. Thatcher. "His name was Aesop. He has been known down through history as the greatest of all fable tellers. For 2600 years, Aesop's reputation has been secure. But, today, a new challenger has appeared on the horizon—the Premier of Saskatchewan. Some of his fables make old Aesop look like a piker."

Thatcher's durable tongue ticked off the government's industrial fables: a $3 million German pipe plant; a $3,500,000 American pipe plant; a $60 million pulp industry; a $10 million pulp mill; a $200,000 mobile home factory; a $2 million blockboard factory; a $30 million sugar beet refinery; a multi-million dollar iron ore development; a $3 million distillery; a petro-chemical industry . . . Mr. Thatcher's collection of twice-told fables took a little time to run through.

"The CCF has been using these deceptive announcements to create the fiction that thousands of new jobs have been created in industry since 1944, under their regime," said the leader of the Liberals. "How in the light of all these fables and fairy tales about new industries, can the people of Saskatchewan have any confidence in any Socialist promises?"

Mr. Douglas and his colleagues in the Legislature have a quick, short and stock reply to Liberals who criticize their record: "What did the Liberals do for the province before we took over? Nothing!"

Aware of their weakness in the area of manufacturing development, the Socialists like to put more emphasis on their achievements in the field of mineral production and the record is quite impressive. From a level of $22 million in 1944, the value of mineral output made a steady advance to a high of more than $200 million in 1961.

Oil, natural gas and uranium made the major contribution to this bumper mineral harvest. Potash production for the first time will add to the value of minerals produced this year. Two large American potash companies together have spent more than $50 million to build refineries and sink mine shafts and other companies are conducting exploration programmes. Saskatchewan contains one of the richest and largest deposits of potash in the world. Mr. Douglas made the prediction that Saskatchewan will become the potash capital of the world, and he could be right.

Charges that the provincial economy has suffered under Socialism might validly be discounted on the grounds of political bias when they come from another party, but the charges unfortunately are borne out by irrefutable, non-partisan facts and figures. Unchallengeable statistics make the charges stick that Saskatchewan has done poorly compared with neighbors who practice and support a free enterprise philosophy.

If Saskatchewan under Socialism was short-changed in the past, the economic signs and portents for the future spell out some bleak prospects for the province. Saskatchewan's economy is being pinched from several directions. Events of the past, events taking place and events pending all will bring new pressure to bear on an economic structure which at best has never been too robust and stable.

These adverse factors at work include the threat of more drought, severe grasshopper infestation, the steady withdrawal of oil and mining companies, population losses, a static industrial situation aggravated by industry's aversion to a climate of high taxation.

The oil play, while it lasted, gave the province's economy a shot in the arm. Exploration and development reached their peak about 1957 and then began to decline. In the spring of 1961, 40 geophysical crews were active in Alberta, 23 in British Columbia, 11 in the North West Territories and one in Saskatchewan.

Oil activity in Saskatchewan started late and the industry admits this was due to its distrust of the political climate. The Douglas government then proceeded to do a number of things not calculated to remove this distrust. It gave its power corpora-tion a complete monopoly of the distribution of natural gas, it made special lease concessions to the co-operatives, and then at a time when the industry was facing marketing problems, the government imposed a one percent road allowance production royalty. Road allowances on freehold land are owned by the Crown and the government said that the oil companies must be extracting a certain amount of crude from under these areas.

The oil companies stayed around long enough to develop proven areas and then they began to leave the province. During the past two years a number of companies have closed or curtailed their office facilities in Regina. Sun Oil Company and Canadian Fina Co. pulled out in the spring of 1962. Shell Oil Company made its departure earlier in the year.

The decline in oil exploration in Saskatchewan has sharply reduced provincial revenues from petroleum and natural gas. These revenues declined from a peak level of $22 million in 1957-58 to an estimated $12 million in 1961-62.

Mineral Resources Minister J. H. Brockelbank at the 1962 session of the Legislature acknowledged that oil activity in the province was in a slump. The minister said a major oil discovery was needed to stimulate exploration work.

A week after Mr. Brockelbank commented on the decline in oil work a large mining company operating in Saskatchewan's Pre-Cambrian northland served notice that it was quitting the province. Kerr-Addison Gold Mines Limited said it had made a firm decision to halt its exploration and development programmes in Saskatchewan and move to Manitoba.

The company explained its reasons for the decision in a statement to the Press:

"Kerr-Addison rode along with the mineral resources department and its unfavorable regulations as long as it could but has finally decided to pull out before becoming completely committed with a production programme. Saskatchewan's royalty rate of 12½ per cent is one of the highest in Canada and constitutes an undue cost burden on exploration and development work."

It was somewhere in Ontario that David Cass-Beggs missed out at the polls but this in no way disqualified him from getting a political handout from the Douglas administration in Saskatchewan. The handout to Cass-Beggs was the job of general manager of the Power Corporation, a job that now pays him $25,000 a year.

The threatened loss of Kerr-Addison Gold Mines Limited gave the Saskatchewan Government a bad jolt and sent Mineral Resources Minister Brockelbank hurrying north on a mission of appeasement. A few days later in the Legislature, looking much relieved, Mr. Brockelbank was able to announce that Kerr-Addison had reconsidered its decision to move and would resume exploration work in Saskatchewan. The government, the minister disclosed, had given the company assurances that the mineral disposition regulations would be altered to make them more favorable to mining companies.

This crisis was no sooner resolved than bad news arrived from Ottawa. This time it was the possibility of a shutdown of the big Beaverlodge uranium mine of Crown-owned Eldorado Mining and Smelting Ltd. The news report said the mine probably would halt operations by September, 1964. With other uranium mines already closed, Saskatchewan's once thriving uranium industry appeared to be going out of business—at least until new markets could be found for the province's rich deposits of radio-active ore.

That all was not well with northern development, was revealed by the government itself during the 1962 session of the Legislature. Information tabled at the request of the Liberal opposition disclosed that mines producing uranium, copper or zinc had dwindled to four from a peak of 30 operating in 1959. Twelve of these operations had been discontinued between 1960 and 1961.

And trouble was brewing along the Saskatchewan-Manitoba border. Saskatchewan merchants complained to the government that residents of the province living near the border were going into Manitoba to do their shopping to avoid paying Saskatchewan's five per cent sales tax. This was the tax that was increased from three to five per cent to help defray the costs of the medical care plan that Mr. Douglas rushed into law before he left to lead the NDP. Border town merchants on the Saskatchewan side blamed the government and its sales tax for their loss of business and they were demanding action.

Drought is another grim prospect the province has to contend with. Rainless skies and burning suns destroyed Saskatchewan's 1961 wheat crop and the economy felt the blow. If drought conditions are prolonged the economic loss could be critical for farmer, business and government. Grasshoppers, familiar pestilence of the dry Thirties, present another major threat to the grain crops.

Population decline in the province is another symptom of Saskatchewan's economic troubles. Census figures for 1961 issued by the Dominion Bureau of Statistics disclosed that the most general and widespread population losses in Canada occurred in nine of Saskatchewan's 18 census divisions. The four major cities of the province recorded increases.

Against this backdrop of gathering clouds on the province's economic horizons, the government in March, 1962, introduced the largest spending programme in Saskatchewan's history. The CCF budget called for expenditures of $174 million. The last Liberal budget before the Socialists took office totalled $24 million.

It was a budget that provided for more welfare measures and more taxation. It was a Socialist government's rather strange fiscal approach to the problem of an ailing economy, the likelihood of another year of drought and the prospect of diminishing revenues.

8

The Political Machine

THE SASKATCHEWAN Socialists have
won five provincial elections and the mystery thereof is who
voted for them. The morning after the CCF victory at the polls
it is never possible to find a citizen who admits to voting for any
party but the Liberals or the Conservatives. The CCF voter
seems to be completely non-existent.

Whoever it is that marks the ballots for the CCF—gremlin
or poltergeist—there is no mystery about the methods the party
employs to win elections. The CCF political machine is a big,
smooth 12-cylinder model fueled by patronage.

The political machine is not the patented invention of
Tommy Douglas. Government from the time of the Caesars
had had its quota of political hucksters and back room boys.
Nor is there anything unusual about a government employee
trying to protect a regular pay cheque by doing a little vote
hustling for his employers.

But there is some irony in the fact that a political party
which conducted its first election campaign like a religious
crusade and made its declamations sound like the Sermon
on the Mount, should then proceed to use the public purse
to build what other political parties have called the most
formidable political machine in Canada.

Ross Thatcher, leader of the Saskatchewan Liberals, has a
great deal of respect for the power and persuasion of the CCF
political organization. As a former member of that party, he has

intimate knowledge of how it is constituted and how it works. Addressing the Liberal provincial convention in December, 1961, Mr. Thatcher warned that his party would not find it easy to dislodge the entrenched Socialists. Said the Liberal leader:

"Let us not forget we face one of the most formidable political machines in the western world. Let no one make the mistake of thinking the Socialists are a pushover. They have a machine built on patronage, employing civil servants in party organizations, and one well heeled and opulent with financial resources."

The CCF machine has neither the crudity of the old Huey Long porkbarrelocracy nor the violence of the Duplessis press gangs. It could give both Louisiana and Quebec lessons in the gentle art of finagling the vote. Organization meticulous as the execution of a battle plan is the spark plug of the machine. It pulls in the votes at tea parties, picnics, bingo games and dances. Its apostles do their work in the council chambers of municipal government, in labor unions, in schools and churches, in co-operative organizations, in farmyard and factory.

The active workers of the party are a mixture of dedicated men and women and those whose piety goes no deeper than a pay cheque. The shock troops of the organization are recruited under a patronage system which places them on the payrolls of the Civil Service and the Crown Corporations. The system has gathered in faithful party workers from the early days of the movement, defeated CCF MLA's and MP's, unsuccessful candidates, friends and relatives of cabinet ministers, and a motley crowd of textbook Socialists looking for jobs and the chance to share in the spoils of victory when the revolution liberates all of Canada from the economic thralldom of Capitalism.

The Douglas political machine in Saskatchewan built up rapidly after the CCF came to power in 1944. CCF election posters proclaiming an end to political patronage and promising that the Socialists would keep politics out of the Civil Service were still decorating rural telephone poles and the windows of CCF committee rooms, when Mr. Douglas set about the task of using the public service to expand his political organization.

Throughout the 1944 election campaign CCF candidates raised a terrific din over the sinful practice of patronage and politics in government service and vowed that there would be none of this skulduggery in a CCF Civil Service.

Mr. Douglas in a campaign address in Regina in June, 1944, said the CCF "aims to have clean and honest government". This would be accomplished by doing away with party patronage in the Civil Service and by setting up a purchasing board in Saskatchewan.

The Premier made good on his word to set up a purchasing board. He appointed to head the board the man who stepped down as CCF candidate in Weyburn to let Mr. Douglas contest the seat.

The CCF party organ, the Commonwealth, also joined the chorus of CCF voices condemning patronage and promising there would be an end to it under the CCF. Said the Commonwealth in its edition of May 31, 1944, "A CCF government will abolish patronage by setting up a genuine Civil Service Commission."

Mr. Douglas set up his "genuine Civil Service Commission" by appointing a Commission of one. The Commissioner was a school teacher from Moose Jaw who coincidentally was also president of the Moose Jaw CCF Association.

The national leader of the party, able, earnest M. J. Coldwell, also made a contribution to the campaign orations on the subject of a chaste and honest Civil Service. Addressing an audience at Saskatoon on June 9, 1944, Mr. Coldwell said:

"The day of the political heeler in Saskatchewan will be at an end if the CCF is elected. I would sever my connection with the party if it were not so."

Fortunately, Mr. Coldwell chose to ignore the shenanigans of his colleagues in Saskatchewan and continued to do his job in Ottawa until he lost his seat in the 1958 election.

The Civil Service was mentioned again when Mr. Douglas delivered a speech on May 26, 1944, in his home constituency of Weyburn. He pledged that a CCF government would establish a non-political Civil Service to hire and also promote on the basis of merit only. And on this occasion he served warning that marked for dismissal when the CCF took office was a certain deputy minister who had taken leave of absence to campaign for the Liberal party.

This deputy minister whose head was slated to go on the CCF chopping block was a rare fellow, indeed. Rare in the sense that he removed himself from the public payroll before engaging in politics. This little mark of deference to the taxpayer seemed to go out of vogue after 1944. If it were to come back into fashion, a large number of government employees would be off the public payroll permanently.

Mr. Douglas in 1944 found political cause for the dismissal of one Liberal deputy minister. The government that takes over from the CCF will have a great deal more house cleaning to do than that. A new government would probably be justified in getting rid of not one but five or six deputy ministers. The new broom—unless it is uncommonly magnanimous—will also have the job of sweeping out a string of directors and other lesser lights who play political pinochle on the taxpayer's time.

The CCF since the start of the movement in the Thirties taught the old parties a thing or two about machine organization. The 1944 election campaign demonstrated the thorough and methodical work of the party in building a political machine. And it was all done mainly by voluntary effort and the nickels and dimes of its supporters, and in the Thirties even nickels and dimes were scarce.

CCF devices for mobilizing and maintaining a political apparatus are not unlike the methods used in totalitarian countries to indoctrinate the workers. The CCF goes in strong for study sessions for the memberships of its community clubs. Speakers address the clubs on party philosophy; national and international events of political significance are discussed and debated; party strategy and organization on the local level come in for attention. The provincial headquarters of the CCF keeps the local organizations well supplied with printed literature on party activities, political news and inspirational messages on CCF aims and objectives.

The useful role of young people in a political organization was not overlooked by the CCF. The party's Cooperative Commonwealth Youth Movement is an effective arm of the machine. Educational and recreational programmes for the membership go on winter and summer. The young people get an intensive training in party policy and programme. The youth movement has representation on the provincial council of the party and it makes its influence felt at CCF conventions.

Heart of the CCF political organization is the provincial headquarters in Regina. Field organizers work out of the Regina office and maintain liaison with local poll organizations, constituency associations and the community clubs.

A former organizer for the CCF said a great deal of the success of the party organization was due to the work of women supporters:

"The CCF provincially has more active women workers than either of the two old parties. There has always been a sort of 'underdog' appeal about the CCF that won the sympathy of the ladies and the party was shrewd enough to see this and use it. Some of the party's best organizers are women. They can be pretty sharp at the business of politics, too. The old parties miss a bet not recruiting more of them for the work of organization."

The distaff side of the party organized the dances, whist parties, bazaars and rummage sales that brought in the nickels and dimes to keep the machine operating. After it came to power, the CCF continued to foster the image of a party with patches in its pants and holes in its socks subsisting on small change from the pockets of farmer and worker, while business poured big money into the coffers of the old parties. The CCF said it wanted no part of this tainted money, anyway. It was content to struggle along on the pennies of honest sweat and toil.

Although it expressed these sentiments publicly, privately the party showed no particular aversion to accepting some of this tainted money and in not inconsiderable amounts. Business sometimes found it useful to seek the goodwill of the government by making a gift to party funds. The scent of profit occasionally anaesthetized a difference of political belief and the CCF found allies and financial support in rather unexpected places. The government's Industrial Development Fund had its uses in changing political thought and allegiance.

For a party that subsisted on the pennies of honest sweat and toil, the CCF is surprisingly affluent when it comes to financing an election campaign. Mr. Douglas hailed the results of the 1960 election as a "miracle" victory for the CCF. The inference was that despite the pelf and Press power mustered against it by the other parties, the Socialists had won out with no other resources but the nickels and dimes of the poor.

The disclosure of election expenditures suggested that more than nickels and dimes had miraculously come to the aid of the party. The CCF in that 1960 election year poured out a total of $223,786 on TV programmes, radio propaganda, newspaper advertisements and other election-winning devices.

The nickels and dimes were in plentiful supply, too, when the CCF opened its campaign in the 1961 Weyburn by-election. In an effort to keep Mr. Douglas' old seat in the CCF fold, the party spent almost twice as much as the Liberals but lost the election anyway. CCF-NDP expenses for Oran Reiman's campaign amounted to $7049, while the Liberal bill for J. H. Staveley's successful bid totalled $3617.

Effective as the party's political organization was before it came to power, the CCF once elected found itself with a potent new weapon—patronage. The apparatus of government grew rapidly under Socialism and the party's camp followers moved in. To make sure that no political infidels slipped by in the guise of Socialists, the government appointed as chief scrutineer and screener a public service commissioner who had satisfactorily demonstrated his loyalty in the holy crusade against Capitalism. He subsequently left the service of the CCF to take a better paying job with a Capitalist organization.

The public service commission made one appearance before a microphone to frankly discuss its function and set at rest suspicions that it was guilty of patronage and political favoritism. An unidentified voice posed the questions and the members of the commission supplied the answers. The performance finally reached the final and key question: Did the government ever attempt to influence the commission in selecting personnel for the Civil Service? Never, said the commission vehemently. It was quite a good show until the unknown interrogator was identified. He turned out to be the deputy minister of the government's information department, son-in-law of a cabinet minister and former business partner of a member of the CCF provincial executive. This circumstance rather tended to spoil what had been quite a convincing performance.

Another major centre of CCF political activity is the government's Crown Corporation structure. The Corporations in the 1961-62 fiscal year employed 5600 workers and their combined payrolls amounted to $26,500,000. These enterprises do provide a lot of jobs for citizens of the province but payrolls and jobs on this magnitude place in the hands of a government a powerful instrument for political use. Patronage quite openly operates throughout the Crown Corporations. Personnel, especially on management level, labor assiduously to preserve and perpetuate the CCF in office. It is a matter of self-preservation, too, for some of these enterprises of dubious value would probably disappear under a more business-like administration.

Most politically active of the Crown Corporations is the Saskatchewan Power Corporation. Its general manager is a Fabian Socialist from England and an unsuccessful CCF candidate in Ontario. The government pays him $25,000 a year to run the big and growing power utility and its monopoly natural gas division. Along with the distribution of gas and the production of power, the Corporation also generates a great volume of propaganda thinly disguised as news releases. Indoctrinated personnel of the Corporation range across the province at election time to perform a variety of chores designed to do the government some good at the polls. The minister in charge of the Corporation is a former party organizer.

The Power Corporation is a big and lavish spender. Its elaborate publicity department—headed by an ex-sanitary engineer—is short on journalistic experience but long on political loyalty. The high-salaried department cultivates the underpaid minions of the daily press and overawes them with the splendor and hospitality of the Corporation's frequent press junkets, gas turning-on ceremonies and parties, conferences, conventions, information tours and other assorted convivial occasions. The Corporation does things on a grand scale—even its debt is monumental, $350 million and growing at the rate of $40 million to $50 million annually.

In the process of accumulating this debt, the Corporation did help to bring some badly needed industries to the province. Large-scale programmes of rural electrification and gas distribution were mainly responsible for attracting a steel pipe plant, a transformer factory, a wire and cable industry and other smaller manufacturing and service industries. Saskatchewan's construction industry also is a beneficiary of the Corporation's mushrooming growth. Warehouse, thermal and hydro power projects and a $6 million headquarters building in Regina have done much to maintain building values at high levels.

Critics of Corporation policy contend that it has over-extended itself and is heading into deep financial trouble. Whether or not this is true, there are signs that the utility plans to put the brakes on for a while. What effect this will have on the future of the new industries it helps in a large way to support, is a question that only time will answer.

Although political patronage in the CCF Civil Service is no more of a secret than Elizabeth Taylor's marital troubles, the government automatically comes out with a flat denial when any such thing is suggested. Charges by Liberal members that droves of political heelers are roosting on the public payroll bring from the government the solemn declaration that "only us chickens are here, boss".

When the opposition occasionally gets mean and confronts the government with names, positions and salaries, the government loses some of its composure and retorts that the Liberals have no reason to talk. What about the Jimmy Gardiner political machine?

Defeated CCF candidates, provincially and federally, have never had to apply for unemployment insurance. Mr. Douglas charitably found jobs for them somewhere in government service. The Liberals did some research in this particular field of patronage and produced some vital statistics on the incidence of ex-politicians on the public payroll. The roster of government job handouts compiled by the Liberals goes back to 1944, the year Mr. Douglas was promising there would be an end to political patronage once the CCF was elected.

The 1944 election was scarcely over when the province's new premier began dispensing patronage. The first recipient of political dole was E. T. Stinson of Weyburn. Mr. Douglas appointed Mr. Stinson to head the government's new Purchasing Agency. Mr. Stinson was certainly entitled to a government job of some kind, for he had obligingly resigned as CCF candidate in Weyburn to let Mr. Douglas contest the seat and win it. This sacrifice of Stinson's provided Douglas with a steady job for seventeen years and the least Douglas could do in return was find a job for Mr. Stinson.

T. J. Bentley, CCF member of Parliament for Swift Current, was defeated in the 1949 federal election and the Douglas government promptly came to his rescue and appointed him Director of Staff Training. Mr. Bentley was successful in a bid to win a provincial seat and with it a Cabinet post as Minister of Social Welfare.

H. A. Bryson, MP for Humboldt-Melfort, was one of the Prairie politicians flattened by the Diefenbaker steam-roller in 1958. Mr. Bryson sent word along to Regina that he was jobless and the Douglas Employment Agency fixed a place for him on the public payroll as a Co-operative Management Advisor.

Yorkton MP G. H. Castleden struck out as a politician in the 1949 federal election but it was some months after this before he made his appearance on the government payroll. Mr. Castleden succeeded Mr. Bentley as Director of Staff Training when Bentley won a seat in the provincial legislature.

It was somewhere in Ontario that David Cass-Beggs missed out at the polls but this in no way disqualified him from getting a political handout from the Douglas administration in Saskatchewan. The handout to Cass-Beggs was the job of general manager of the Power Corporation, a job that now pays him $25,000 a year. Mr. Cass-Beggs seems well-qualified for his job. He holds science and engineering degrees and he was an associate professor in electrical engineering at the University of Toronto and a professor in electrical engineering at University College, Swansea.

The defeated CCF member of the Legislature for Souris-Estevan, C. D. Cuming, was given the post of sheriff at Estevan. N. Buchannan, who represented Notokue-Willowbunch in the Legislature from 1944 to 1956, was placed on the payroll of the Power Corporation.

A. D. Connon, MLA for the Battlefords, was defeated in

the 1948 provincial election and the government appointed him commissioner of the Workmen's Compensation Board. For its chairman, the Board got Social Welfare Minister O. W. Valleau after his elimination in the provincial election of 1948.

One defeated MLA who appears to have been short-changed when Douglas was passing out the patronage is Dmy-tro Zipchen, a former CCF member for Redberry. According to the record, Dmytro was sloughed off with the job of vendor in a government liquor store at Hafford. Mr. Zipchen seems to have been discriminated against both in the matter of position and salary. The other explanation is that Dmytro was just unlucky enough to need a job at a time when the supply was temporarily depleted.

The government did better by J. A. Young, member of the Legislature for Biggar from 1938 to 1944. Mr. Young was appointed Superintendent of Insurance in 1945. He was later named Deputy Provincial Treasurer and Registrar under the Security Act.

These are only some of the ex-CCF politicians who were given government jobs under the Douglas patronage system. It would be tedious to go on listing them. And after all, perhaps it was not so grievously wrong to extend patronage to these people. But it was the CCF that condemned patronage as a wicked practice and swore that it would never happen under their administration. Because of this holier-than-thou attitude, the Socialists left themselves wide open to criticism when they went into the business of patronage on a truly grand scale.

Politicians who go down to defeat would seem to be entitled to some consideration from the government they supported. Many of these people give up careers to enter politics, sacrifice family life and often find themselves worse off financially. Campaigning is a tough grind, a drain on nerves and physically exhausting. A government job by way of some recompense for their work and sacrifices would not seem to be too much of an abuse of patronage. In many instances, too, these ex-politicians settle down to their government jobs and retire from political activity.

Patronage of another color and odor is the dispensation of key jobs at fat salaries to droves of political parasites whose real function in the Civil Service is to keep the machine greased and oiled, grind out propaganda, keep an ear cocked for treasonable whisperings among the rank and file of ordinary Civil Servants, and perform a variety of political chores for their government masters. A lot of these people drifted into the province when the CCF took office. The government obligingly found jobs for some of their wives, too. Overlooked was the fact that these positions could have been filled by unemployed ordinary citizens of the province.

One department of government that probably will be thoroughly renovated when the CCF departs is the Department of Industry and Information. This is the propaganda arm of the government. The information branch—its staff is twice the size of any newspaper office in Saskatchewan—churns out a great volume of news releases which deal with the manifold activities of a busy, progressive and efficient government. The industry branch of the department is noted chiefly for its failure to bring any industry to the province. This branch did claim credit for establishing a steel mill in Saskatchewan but the claim was not pressed after the mill threatened to become more of a problem than an asset.

To critics who charged that the information branch was simply a propaganda vehicle of the CCF, Mr. Douglas answered that it performed a useful service in getting the government's story across to a hostile Press. The hostility is there all right but this doesn't stop the newspapers from using large amounts of pro-government copy turned out by the information branch. Most of the pieces unfavorable to the government appear on the editorial pages of the papers. The CCF is not without friends and supporters on news desks and reporting staffs. Probing and digging into government affairs to ferret out information governments would sooner keep to themselves is a legitimate function of newspaper work, but in Saskatchewan it has become a lost art. By and large, and with some exceptions, the Douglas political machine has not had to contend with a very formidable or effectual Press opposition.

CCF ministers every now and again discharge a few rounds at the biased Capitalist Press. Education Minister O. A. Turnbull, during the 1962 session of the Legislature, accused the Press Gallery of writing biased reports of speeches. Mr. Turnbull said members of the Press were obliged to write stories reflecting the editorial point of view of their papers:

"They have the difficult job of making all the speeches we make sound to be redundant, ridiculous and naive and they have the more difficult job of making all the speeches from the left (Liberal side) sound as if they were pearls of wisdom. The people who control the Press, control the point of view of the Press and the reporters. The people who work for the Press, have no choice but to write in the way in which the people who control the Press find it favorable."

The next day in the Legislature, having thought things over in the meantime, Mr. Turnbull rose to tactfully withdraw "any remarks which might reflect on the integrity of the Press Gallery." His remarks, said the minister, were only intended "to draw the relationship between the ownership of paper and the editorial point of view."

The Liberals had their day in court when they levelled charges of political activity by senior government employees and to substantiate these charges they produced a report of a meeting of the Saskatchewan CCF Publicity Advisory Committee. Listed as committee members were such people as the deputy minister of Municipal Affairs, the secretary of the Economic Advisory and Planning Board, the associate deputy minister of Industry and Information, the clerk of the Executive Council, the executive director of the South Saskatchewan

River Development Commission, the director of Photographic Services (subsequently director of publicity for the Industrial Office), and Mr. Douglas' confidential Boswell and unofficial press secretary, Christopher Higginbotham.

The Liberals focussed their attention on the associate deputy minister of Industry and Information, Tom Hill, and Mr. Higginbotham. The Liberals said the pair should get off the public payroll if they were doing publicity work for the CCF.

Mr. Hill denied that he was a member of the CCF publicity committee and said his name had been used without permission. In Mr. Hill's case this was probably true. The associate deputy spends most of his time away from Regina, touring the North American continent on vague goodwill missions for the Government of Saskatchewan.

Mr. Higginbotham answered the charges by issuing a lengthy statement in which he denied any affiliation with the CCF and declared that he had never written publicity for any party or worked for any party. Higginbotham does a weekly radio program on provincial affairs and his pay for this work comes from the information branch of the Department of Industry and Information. The Liberals noted that for this work the government in 1961 paid Higginbotham $6,132.

Mr. Higginbotham calls himself a free lance writer. He has been a habitue of the Legislative Building for almost as long as the CCF have been there. He makes his headquarters the year round in the Press Gallery office but his favorite roosting place was Mr. Douglas' office when he was premier. Higginbotham is Regina correspondent for Time Magazine and the CBC. He also writes for "Information", the official organ of the United Steelworkers of America. A Higginbotham story in the February, 1962, edition of the magazine appropriately enough was on the subject of Tommy Douglas. Of Douglas, he wrote:

"Tommy Douglas is now blazing new trails in Canada. His philosophy and convictions haven't changed down the years.

He is still the same orator, thinker and practical humanitarian who organized the unemployed and farmers in the drought and depression in Saskatchewan of the 1930's. He believes with unremitting conviction that intelligent social and economic planning can relieve suffering and want nationally and globally."

It was Higginbotham who persuaded Douglas to put the highlights of his political career on tape. Higginbotham operated the recording machine and prodded Douglas' memory with questions. The project was carried on at intervals over a period of several months. When Mr. Douglas was named leader of the NDP, Higginbotham suggested that this would be the time to do a book on Douglas' life, using the taped recording. Douglas agreed and then there was the matter of settling on a writer who would deal with Douglas sympathetically. The pair decided it should be Jack Scott, columnist for the Vancouver Sun, who had written a series of glowing articles on Douglas during the 1960 election campaign.

Higginbotham got in touch with Scott and Scott was willing. He arranged to get leave of absence from his paper and then brought up the question of a $5000 advance to pay his expenses while the book was being written. Douglas said this could be arranged through the NDP, but for some reason the money was not forthcoming and the book project was abandoned.

Whatever its other faults, the government of Tommy Douglas was good to the people on the public payroll who kept the party machine functioning smoothly. It gave them good salaried positions and comfortable private offices, it provided them with government cars to drive and it made a generous provision in the budgets for travelling expenses.

Public servants of the unprivileged genus snidely call the Department of Industry and Information the Department of Vacations Unlimited. So-called business trips on expense accounts in total at the end of a fiscal year read like the log of a global luxury cruise. One notorious free-loader in a four-year period made it to Ceylon, Japan and twice to Britain and the Continent.

Trips by ministers and Civil Servants at the taxpayers' expense drew some sharp words from Liberal Leader Ross Thatcher during the 1961 session of the Legislature:

"In passing, Mr. Speaker, there is one more Socialist habit I feel I should comment on—the practice of cabinet ministers and top civil servants taking trips overseas and elsewhere, at the taxpayers' expense. Repeatedly during the past decade, ministers have made these jaunts using as an excuse the suggestion that they were searching for new industries. But the new industries never seem to arrive. Travelling to promote industry is perhaps in some cases desirable, but where these trips yield nothing but propaganda and free vacations, it is high time this free-loading was stopped. The tax burden on the people of Saskatchewan is heavy enough without paying the expenses of luxury vacations abroad for cabinet ministers and their political friends in the government."

For a party that likes to advertise its working-class background and talk about its frugal nickel-and-dime climb to power, the CCF after it got control of the public treasury quite quickly shed the threadbare garment of austerity and acquired an appetite for Capitalist pleasures and luxuries on expense accounts, of course. This high-living has been more pronounced in recent years. The cynical suggest that government ministers are reading the signs of a soon-to-come return to beans and hamburger.

One of the useful cogs in the CCF political machine is the Economic Advisory and Planning Board. This department turns out statistical propaganda for the government—facts and figures on population, profits, production, etc. which can always manage to present a brighter Saskatchewan picture than results from a study of Dominion Bureau of Statistics reports. The Board is a training school for young Socialist economists who graduate and move on to responsible positions in other departments of government. Head of this section is a shrewd little Japanese-Canadian, T. K. Shoyama. Mr. Shoyama was granted leave of absence early in 1962 to put his talents at the service of Mr. Douglas and the NDP.

The government of Saskatchewan is one of the province's largest advertisers and this puts another influential weapon in its hand. A pro-government advertising committee meets periodically to decide how much will be spent in various papers and magazines and woe betide the publication that has printed something unflattering about the CCF government. The chances are good this publication will get nothing. The boycott will remain in force long enough to drive home the lesson or until a space salesman shows up to apologize or to reason against the cut. The Financial Post was off the list for almost a year after it ran an adverse article on the CCF Crown Corporations.

Patronage in the CCF is not restricted to job handouts. A large slice of the government's advertising is turned over to a political friend who runs an ad agency in Regina. George Bothwell of the Bothwell Advertising Co. is on the CCF-NDP executive and is director of publicity for the Saskatchewan party. Mr. Bothwell opened his agency after the CCF came to power.

Whenever Mr. Bothwell decides his agency needs more business he pays a visit to one of his friends in the cabinet and makes his request. The minister obligingly picks up the telephone and passes the word along to the advertising committee. The committee obediently takes this business away from the other Regina agency and transfers it to Mr. Bothwell's agency.

The second agency—an old established firm in the city— lost $50,000 worth of government business in a period of a few days in 1961. This business went to the Bothwell agency, too. When a representative of the other firm protested to the Minister of Industry and Information he was informed that his firm was being disciplined for having someone on the staff who was unfriendly to the CCF. Freedom of political activity in Saskatchewan is not something that should be taken too literally, especially by those who are exposed to economic reprisal by the government.

One of the minor cogs in the CCF political machine is a public servant who functions as an organizer during election campaigns and the rest of the time occupies a government office with a sign on the door which identifies him as the Director of Public Relations. In this capacity (according to Civil Servants who study his habits) he reads pocket books and clips magazines. His secretary knits.

Observers of this interesting study in "patronage quiescent" report that briefly twice daily, morning and afternoon, there is a burst of activity in the Director's office. This action comes when the Director puts his pocket book down on the desk, rises with decision, strides to the door of his office, opens it, and runs down the 20 feet of corridor to the bathroom. He returns on the run, retrieves the book and the action is over for the morning. There was a period when he was given an assistant director. The assistant sat outside with the secretary. The secretary knitted. The Director read his pocket book and the assistant studied a seed catalogue.

The Director finally developed a project. The secretary put her knitting aside and typed out a memo addressed to the cabinet. It was a suggestion for improving the public relations of Civil Servants who answer telephones. It was an ingenious plan. A crew of eavesdroppers would circulate through government offices, listen in on secretaries and stenographers using the telephone and check them for courtesy, personality and diction. It was a good idea until the Press got hold of it and turned it into a script for a Mack Sennett comedy.

The Director went back to reading his pocket books to find inspiration for another project. He was still reading when another election rolled around. Now at hand was the work he was hired to do. The government replaced his car with a new one and he was off to the hustings to do some organizing for the party.

Patronage is not difficult to find in the CCF. Liberals going over public accounts during the 1962 sitting of the Legislature came across the name of Premier Lloyd's brother. He was listed as a special field representative for the Department of Co-operation and Co-operative Development at a salary of $8364. The Liberals demanded his dismissal.

Wilfred Gardiner (L-Melville), son of the late James Gardiner, moved that Mr. Lloyd be fired because "his service can only be for political purposes and devoted to the establishment of Socialist principles which are diametrically opposed to co-operative principles."

CCF Committee Chairman John Thiessen refused to accept Mr. Gardiner's motion. He said the committee would not deal with any motion until the study of public accounts had been completed. It is not likely that Mr. Lloyd will find himself unemployed. The CCF majority in the Legislature easily takes care of these situations.

One of Mr. Douglas' major speeches before he left to lead the NDP was delivered in the Debate on the Speech from the Throne after opening of the Legislature in 1960. The speech was entitled "More Abundant Living" and it was the slogan the party used during the 1960 election campaign.

In this speech the Premier quoted at length from a study of Resources and Industrial Opportunities for the Province of Saskatchewan, prepared by the Stanford Research Institute:

"This (report) was undertaken by the Stanford Research Institute in conjuction with the Economic Research Corporation of Montreal and Sandwell & Company Limited of Vancouver, B.C. We selected the Stanford Research Institute because they are probably the biggest and best known industrial and economic consultants in the world. They have done research and survey work for almost every large corporation on the North American continent. They are noted for being somewhat cautious and conservative but this is an advantage because the value of this report, apart from its recommendations to the government, is the fact that we propose to put it into the hands of investors and industrialists in Canada, the United States, Great Britain and other countries of the world. With the reputation that this company has, we feel that the report will get a very good hearing."

Mr. Douglas went on to quote selected paragraphs from the report:

"In the last ten years (1948-58) mining production has almost quadrupled in value, while that of the construction industry has tripled. The net value contributed by the manu- facturing sector has increased by more than two and one-half times."

He then read what the Stanford Research Report had to say about the social climate in Saskatchewan:

"In summary there can be no doubt that the activities of the provincial government, both direct and indirect, to stimulate economic activity through encouragement of private industry, assistance to cooperatives and Crown Corporations, and the creation of an environment designed to increase the national welfare of the people and be conducive to business operations, have met with success."

And after quoting several paragraphs which built up an image of Saskatchewan flourishing in the present and mov- ing toward an even more glorious future, Mr. Douglas com- mented:

"That, I think, sums up very well the view which the Stanford Research Institute takes with reference to Saskat- chewan's future possibilities and opportunities.

The Premier's statement was not quite right in one respect. The Stanford Research Institute had not exactly arrived at this view all by itself. In naming the authors of the report

[163]

Mr. Douglas overlooked mentioning Saskatchewan's Economic Advisory and Planning Board, the Industrial Development Office, the Mineral Resources Department, and a few others.

The Premier also omitted to mention that a first report prepared by the Stanford Research Institute had not been found acceptable by the Government of Saskatchewan. In his remarks in the Legislature Mr. Douglas said the Stanford Research Institute "are noted for being somewhat cautious and conservative." The first report was just too much so to suit the government. But with some helpful suggestions, revisions, deletions, additions and a little ghost-writing by the boys in the back room, the Stanford Institute came up with a new view of the province which was nothing like the old view at all. Naturally the government was surprised and delighted. They said Stanford had done a wonderful job. The first report was quietly spirited away and seen no more.

The Stanford Report, quite by chance of course, made its appearance in nice time for the 1960 election campaign. In his address to the Legislature on the theme of "More Abundant Living", Mr. Douglas said it was the intention of the government to put copies of the report in the hands of investors and industrialists in Canada, the United States, Great Britain and other countries of the world.

Some of Mr. Douglas' political foes in the 1960 election were just a little suspicious that the Premier was more interested in putting copies of the report in the hands of Saskatchewan voters.

The voters were certainly entitled to copies. It was their $60,000 that paid for the report. One of the nice things about being a government is that you can bill the public treasury for some of your campaign expenses.

9

Labor Legislation

ONE OF THE PARADOXES of Saskatchewan with its pro-labor government and its advanced labor legislation is the fact that it is one of the most difficult provinces in Canada in which to organize workers.

Union organizers publicly acclaim the CCF government for the benefits it has conferred on workers, but privately they wish the government hadn't gone quite so far with its labor legislation. Their jobs would be easier as organizers if the Socialists had left them with a few things they could fight and bargain for with both government and management.

An aggrieved ex-organizer made no bones about the fact that the CCF government has made things tough for union recruiters who earn their pay cheques persuading workers to join trade unions:

"Union organizers in other provinces think we have a picnic here because we've got a pro-labor Santa Claus in the Legislative Building. Talk to workers about organizing and they say: 'Why do we need a union? The government takes care of us!' Not only is it tough to organize workers, it's becoming a problem to hang on to the unions we've got. With the government providing for them, they don't think they're getting value for their union dues. And they're probably right."

The Socialists have put much attractive labor legislation on the statute books. Union leaders in other parts of Canada, their eyes glistening, hail Saskatchewan as the show window of the nation for its enlightened labor laws. As a party claiming to be the champion of labor, and under some pressure by the unions to prove it, it was to be expected that the CCF would make an effort to blazon forth with something bigger and better.

In the department of things bigger and better, the government gave Saskatchewan workers the highest weekly minimum wage rate in Canada—$32. Or at least it was the highest until Alberta in 1961 increased that province's minimum wage to $34. The Saskatchewan rate for workers 18 years and under is $30, ahead of Alberta by $4. The CCF also took the lead in Workmen's Compensation rates and eliminated waiting periods. The province's Annual Holidays Act entitles every employee to two weeks' vacation with pay and after five accumulated years of employment, three weeks. None of the other provinces makes provision for a three weeks' vacation.

Saskatchewan was more generous than the other provinces in fixing pay regulations governing public holidays. Full-time employees who do not work on any of eight specified public holidays receive their regular pay. If required to work on a holiday, employees in all workplaces except hotels, restaurants, hospitals, nursing homes and educational institutions must be paid, in addition to their regular pay for the holiday, time and one-half the regular rate for every hour or part of an hour worked. This means the employee receives two and one-half times his regular pay.

Other full-time employees excluded from this ruling who work on holidays receive, in addition to their regular pay, wages at the regular rate or, in lieu of this, equivalent time off at regular pay rates.

Manitoba is the only other province that makes specific provision for holiday or alternative compensation. Employees working on seven general holidays are entitled to time and one-half their regular rate of pay.

In a speech at Powell River, B.C., some years ago, Mr. Douglas reviewed the CCF program for "Security". Along the way, he made brief mention of Saskatchewan's Trade Union Act. These were his words:

"Next we tried to afford some security to the worker. The Trade Union Act was passed. Every union worker has the right by law to associate with his fellow workers for the purpose of bargaining collectively with his employer. It is mandatory that the employer bargain with his employees. It is a criminal offence in Saskatchewan for an employer not to bargain, to have a company union or to fire a man."

Although it sounded very much like it, it is safe to assume that the Premier of Saskatchewan did not intend to imply that the province's Trade Union Act took away the right of management to fire a man for good reason. This assumption, however, would not get much support from employers who have come up against the administration of the Act. Regardless of the cause for dismissal, in Saskatchewan it can be quite a difficult matter to remove a union member from a company payroll.

In large ways and in many small ways, the province's labor legislation—from the point of view of the employee—appears to be just about the best to be found in Canada and in many industrial areas of the United States.

Saskatchewan with all these glossy labor statutes on its books should look like Labor's Land of Promise to workers less fortunately endowed in other parts of the country.

As the worker's Mecca, it might have been expected to attract a great flow of migrants from those places where Trade Union Acts are less aggressive in protecting the rights of labor.

But this stampede of workers to Saskatchewan has not come about yet. Oddly enough, it has been the other way around. Working people of the province in quite substantial numbers over a long period of time have been turning their backs on this show window of labor legislation and wending their way by road and rail and air to other parts of Canada where there is less show and more jobs.

The working people of the province have no fault to find with their government's labor laws. But they do wish it were possible for the government to pass a law which would bring more industries to the province and with them more jobs and payrolls. Unemployed workers with rent to pay and mouths to feed derive little comfort from the provisions of the Annual Holidays Act or the Trade Union Act.

Saskatchewan's Trade Union Act is quite a good piece of legislation. But the interpretation and administration of its provisions are something else again. Executor of these provisions is the province's Labor Relations Board and the impartiality of this Board in the view of management is more fiction than fact.

Employers of labor in Saskatchewan take the view that the government forced its advanced labor legislation on management too quickly. They contend that this has put an excessive burden of cost on their operations and hurt the competitive position of local industry. But unhappy about it though they might be, they'd probably only have grumbled and accepted the situation had it not been for a Labor Relations Board whose union-leaning judgments and decisions sometimes make them hopping mad. As a consequence, management in Saskatchewan is an armed camp marshalled against the Board, the CCF government and the Trade Union Act.

The free enterprise community in Saskatchewan charges that the Socialist policies of the government, high taxation, burdensome labor legislation and the union-favoritism of the Labor Relations Board, create a climate which keeps industry out of the province. The complaint is also made that this bias shown by the Board works to the disadvantage of the individual worker, too.

This is the view advanced by the Rev. H. G. Grant, minister of an Anglican church in Regina, who writes and speaks on the subject of compulsion vs. voluntariness in matters affecting industrial and human relations. The Rev. Grant is an eloquent champion of free competitive enterprise and individual initiative. And being such, naturally he would not see very much that was good in Socialism. The Regina cleric made this comment on Saskatchewan's labor legislation:

"Labor law here in Saskatchewan is not for the workers, the way it is being interpreted by a government appointed Labor Relations Board. It is for unions. In many instances workers have gone on record saying they did not want to be represented by a certain union, but they have had that union foisted off on them despite their petitions and sworn statements."

The Rev. Mr. Grant's statement that the Labor Relations Board "is for unions", would probably not go down too well with the aggrieved ex-organizer who complained that labor legislation in Saskatchewan was making it tough for unions to survive.

This sentiment is voiced by other union officials in the province, but *sotto voce*, of course. Criticism of Tommy Douglas' labor legislation would not be appreciated by the union bosses of the NDP. Nevertheless, Douglas' labor laws do appear to be making it difficult for union recruiters to do business in Saskatchewan.

The organ of the Saskatchewan Industrial Relations Association—a management group—examined the situation and commented:

"Labor laws in Saskatchewan have almost reached the point where unions can offer no real advantage to employees. Union organizers, under the present Trade Union and Labor Acts, have become virtual figureheads. The real power to bargain collectively has been taken away from them and placed in the hands of an all-powerful Labor Relations Board, which in turn stands behind a bulwark of labor legislation in the form of various Acts, Rules and regulations.

"In effect, it amounts to automated collective bargaining in the sense that effective negotiation between employer and employees has become a thing of the past. In almost every instance today, government officials or appointed Boards enter the picture before any collective bargaining agreement is finalized. By taking away the right and the need for responsible bargaining between employer and employees, the need for union representation has also been taken away."

The other political parties in the province, uninhibited in their criticism of most areas of government performance, tread lightly around the question of policy on CCF labor laws. They admit that some changes will be made, but they add the assurance that the legitimate rights of labor will be protected.

Ross Thatcher, chief spokesman for the Liberals, served notice that a Liberal government would make some alterations in existing labor legislation, when he addressed the Regina Builders Exchange in June, 1961.

Mr. Thatcher:

"If we are frank, we must face up to the fact that our labor legislation must be thoroughly overhauled. This should not be taken to mean that I am suggesting turning the clock back, as far as basic trade union rights are concerned.

"However, for too long our provincial government has made Saskatchewan the guinea pig for labor legislation designed mainly to buy Ontario and Quebec trade union votes. Such labor Acts time and again, have cost the province new industries. Many workers are today beginning to realize that fancy labor legislation used mainly for propaganda purposes is no use to the worker without a job. Paper benefits written into statutes are no substitute for job security, efficiency and good wages.

"I believe that labor has every right to ask for its fair share of benefits from industry. But I also believe that industry must operate at a profit before it can share those benefits. Certainly the economic welfare and the job security of our workers must be protected. But there is no justification for labor legislation and regulations which unnecessarily hamstring employers. Far too often this happens in Saskatchewan today. I remind you of some of the decisions of the Labor Relations Board as an example. This Board is probably the most prejudiced in all Canada in its decisions.

"If we expect industry to locate in Saskatchewan and provide jobs, then conditions of employment must be competitive with conditions in Manitoba and Alberta. No one would benefit more from sensible labor legislation than the working people of Saskatchewan. It is this group which would be given jobs by industrialization."

The head of a business which has been established in Saskatchewan for more than twenty years felt that existing labor legislation, with very minor amendments, could be successfully lived with by both employers and employees, if it was administered by a strictly neutral Labor Relations Board.

This employer said that "bureaucratic and biased boards and (labor) department officials harass employers at almost every turn. Companies have left the province rather than put up with such harassment. Others, having explored the situation in advance, have changed their plans and by-passed Saskatchewan to locate in the sister provinces of Manitoba and Alberta."

The Board that gets the dander up of management is composed of seven members: two from labor unions; two representing employers; two named from the public-at-large, and a chairman who frequently casts the deciding vote when the group is split on a decision.

Board chairman appointed by the government is Russian-born P. G. Makaroff, Q.C., a Saskatoon lawyer and a former unsuccessful CCF candidate. The other personnel on the Board in the spring of 1962 were union representatives Fred Mclennan, Saskatoon, president of the Saskatchewan Federation of Labor, and Clarence Lyons, organizer for the Packinghouse Workers Union; employer representatives were Jack Hamilton, a retired lumberman, and George Whitter, personnel manager for the O.K. Economy Stores; public representatives were Mrs. Elsie Hart, past-president of the Ladies organization of the Saskatchewan Farmers Union, and E. Thiesen, secretary of the Farmers Union.

Criticism of biased Board decisions are mainly directed at Chairman Makaroff. These critics, usually employers, complain that in very few instances, regardless of the merits of the case, have decisions been made in favor of an employer or a group of employees opposing a complaint or a request made by a union. The chairman, supported by the two union members and usually by the lone woman representative on the Board, is in a position to influence the decisions of the group. The record of Board decisions does reflect a preponderance in favor of the unions. Because of this evident bias, many employer and employee groups feel that it is a waste of time and money to appear before this tribunal.

One disgruntled businessman complained:

"The chairman of the Board invariably sides with the union representatives whenever there may happen to be an evenly split vote. In many cases, the chairman may have indicated, during the hearing, that he thought an employer or an employee opposing a union claim was justified in his opposition, but nevertheless when the chips are down he votes with the union representatives."

Chairman Makaroff is aware that any union bias he displays as head of the Board will not invite censure from the two top men in Saskatchewan's Department of Labor. Labor Minister C. C. Williams is a dyed-in-the-wool trade unionist and an old-guard Socialist. Mr. Williams was one of Regina's early labor mayors. His deputy minister, H. S. Elkin, was a former union organizer. Mr. Elkin was the target for sharp criticism when a newspaper report of a meeting in Saskatoon disclosed that the deputy minister of labor had addressed the gathering and appealed to it to support the New Democratic Party. This political activity by the deputy brought demands for his resignation. Mr. Williams dismissed the matter as being trivial.

Section 17, Chapter 259, of Saskatchewan's Trade Union Act states: "There shall be no appeal from an order or decision of the (Labor Relations) Board under this Act, and the Board shall have full power to determine any question of fact necessary to its jurisdiction, and its proceeding, orders and decisions shall not be reviewable by any court of law or by any Certiorari, Mandamus, prohibition, injunction or other proceedings whatever."

Section 17 of the Act would appear to invest in the Board the powers of absolute authority and place its decisions beyond the jurisdiction of the courts. But despite this provision, appeals, based on claims that the Board exceeded its powers or acted in a biased manner, have been taken to the courts. And in most instances Board orders have been quashed by court orders.

Unfortunately, the expense of court proceedings have discouraged smaller businessmen from appealing what they felt were unfair decisions from the Board. Usually it is the larger and wealthier companies that take the Labor Relations Board into court. The less well-heeled employer is obliged to live with the Board's decision.

Saskatchewan courts, on occasion, have ripped into the Board for some of its more flagrant exhibitions of bias and abuses of its function. One such instance some years ago was a dispute over certification between the Capital Cab Ltd., Regina, and a union. The cab company protested the union's methods of obtaining employees' signatures and disputed the union's claim that a majority of the employees favored going into the union. The dispute was taken to the Labor Relations Board and the Board ruled in favor of the union. Convinced of the merits of its case, the cab company challenged the Board order in court. Chief Justice Brown of Court of Queen's Bench reviewed the evidence and delivered some scathing remarks on the Board's conduct of the hearings. The judge referred to an earlier application of the union for certification of the employees of the cab company. This first application of the union had brought to light questionable methods employed in obtaining the signatures of employees.

Said Mr. Justice Brown:

"I would have expected the Board at that time, in the light of the evidence before it, to have asserted itself and demonstrated its independence and effectiveness by denouncing the methods of misrepresentation and fraud that had been adopted in securing the signatures of employees of the company to the union cards before the Board at that time, and to have advised the representative of the union, present on that occasion, not to again appear before the Board, in so far as this company was concerned, until sufficient time had elapsed to allow the odor engendered from that application to evaporate. The Board was content at that time to advise the union to withdraw its application, on which suggestion it acted. It was made crystal clear to the Board at that time that the union cards, on which that application was based, were valueless. With that background of experience the Board is again, and so soon, asked to consider another application for the same purpose.

"One is amazed," Judge Brown continued, "that an order of judgment of the Board should be made unionizing these employees under such circumstances. There was, as I see it, no semblance of justice or fair play shown in the proceedings before the Board."

If the Board had wanted to be fair, the judge pointed out, it would, of its own motion, "have adopted the ballot system as the simplest, fairest and safest way of settling the matter. If there ever was a case where the ballot should have been used this, in my opinion, is such a case. Was it denied to the company just because the company and its counsel asked to have the matter decided in that way? One is almost forced to think it was. Why is there provision in the Act and in the Board's regulations for deciding matters of this kind by ballot if it is not to be used in such a case as this? I find myself compelled to say that in the light of the material before me, the Board throughout this so-called hearing, utterly failed to display evidence of good faith and fairness and impartiality to either the company or its employees. The Board appeared to act as if it were in league with the union and was determined to unionize the employees whether or not the company or a majority of the employees desired such a result."

Delivering his judgment, Judge Brown said: "It would surely be an outrage to force these men into unionization under such circumstances and I will not, in any way, facilitate such a result. The application is dismissed with costs against the applicants."

But in spite of its lack of success in getting its orders upheld by the courts, and the far from gentle treatment accorded it by the judiciary in the process, the Board continues unperturbed issuing its pro-union orders; and sooner or later a provoked employer decides to seek justice from a higher tribunal and back into court goes the Labor Relations Board.

In a 1961 court decision, Mr. Justice Disbery quashed an order of the Board which refused the request of a group of employees for the removal of their bargaining agent.

Judge Disbery ruled that the Board had "erred in law" in rejecting the employees' application on the grounds that it had not been made within a specified 30-60 day period prior to termination of a one-year collective bargaining agreement.

"It might be argued that it would be somewhat difficult to understand how the desirable aim of stability in labor relations would be advanced by the Board attempting to impose restrictions which would have the result of forcing employees to be represented by a bargaining agent they no longer wanted." Judge Disbery also pointed out that unions should be the servants of their members and not the masters.

The judge ordered a writ of mandamus to be served on the Board "commanding the Board to hear and determine according to law the application" it had rejected. The court also ordered that the employees were to recover the costs of the action from the Labor Relations Board.

Much of Saskatchewan's labor legislation is loaded against the employer and with a biased Labor Relations Board interpreting the Acts, the employer is in double jeopardy. When a union levels a charge of unfair labor practice at an employer, that fellow is usually a gone goose.

The section of the Trade Union Act Section 8, Subsection 1 dealing wtih unfair labor practices puts the employer at a distinct disadvantage. This section says in part: " . . . if an employer or employer's agent discharges an employee from his employment and it is alleged by a trade union that such employer or employer's agent has committed an unfair labor practice within the meaning of this clause, *it shall be presumed unless the contrary is proved, that such employer or employer's agent has discriminated against such employee in regard to tenure of employment with a view to discouraging membership in or activity in or for a labor organization or participation in proceedings under this Act. . . . "*

The wording of this section of the Act would appear to fix guilt until innocence is proved, as opposed to basic British law which presumes innocence until guilt is proved. This reverse onus principle is built into much of Saskatchewan's labor legislation.

The employer could also be in deep trouble who runs afoul of Section 13, Chapter 259, of the Trade Union Act. This section deals with the "Powers to appoint a controller." The section reads: "In addition to any other penalties imposed or remedies provided by this Act, the Lieutenant-Governor in Council, upon application of the Board and upon being satisfied that any employer has wilfully disregarded or disobeyed any order filled by the Board, may appoint a controller to take possession of any business, plant or premises of such employer within Saskatchewan as a going concern and operate the same on behalf of her Majesty until such time as the Lieutenant-Governor in Council is satisfied that upon the return of such business, plant or premises to the employer the order of the Board will be obeyed."

With a Labor Relations Board not noted for showing too much sympathy to employers, the application of this section of the Act could be a disastrous matter for the owner of a thriving business. In effect, the Saskatchewan government could, by order-in-council, take over a going concern at the mere whim of an unfriendly Labor Relations Board. And this could have unhappy consequences in view of the government's lack of success in operating industries of its own. The hapless owner would run the risk of retrieving a business that was wrecked and bankrupt.

The CCF government not long after it came to power expropriated a Prince Albert box factory. By all accounts, this was not a particularly thriving business nor was it in a state of good repair. The owner apparently felt that his finances would be in a state of worse repair if he followed the orders of the Labor Relations Board. So he ignored them and his business was confiscated. The owner probably wasn't too unhappy over its expropriation. He was quite generously compensated for his loss.

Mr. Douglas in a speech in British Columbia a few years after the government acquired the box factory, explained how it had happened:

"People have been told of how we took over a box factory. Why? The government did not want a box factory but this was the situation: This man had a box factory; he had about 63 employees. They had been trying for one year to get him to sign a collective bargaining agreement. The man refused to do so. The Labor Relations Board came to me and said that the Act must be enforced. I wrote to the man. I told him: 'We do not want to do anything without hearing your side of the case. I would like you and your lawyer to come down to meet the Cabinet'. We set a date. Just before it arrived his lawyer called to ask if we could postpone it for two weeks. After a year I did not see what difference two weeks could make, so I agreed. Do you know what he did? He used those two weeks to transfer the factory over to some of his relatives and to fire every man who had joined the union. That is what the government was faced with—men defying the laws of the province. These people who had worked there were out on the street. The government did the only thing it could do. It stepped in and took over the factory and within 45 minutes had signed a collective bargaining agreement. The court decided the amount we should pay, and we are still operating it at a very good profit. It was the first time in the history of Canada that the court had been used to put an employer in his place; they are usually used to put the employees in their place."

Mr. Douglas made that speech in 1949. If, as he said, the plant was operating profitably then, it was not long after this that it ceased to operate profitably. After it accumulated deficits of $350,000, the plant was quietly shut-down and its employees were out on the street again. The government has not been quite so quick to threaten expropriation since.

There is a provision under the CCF Minimum Wage Act, Section 9, Chapter 264, which is viewed with some distrust and suspicion by management in the province.

This section states: "Any person authorized in writing by the minister may require any employer to make within a stated period full disclosure, production or delivery of all records, documents, statements, writings, books, papers, extracts therefrom or copies thereof in his possession or control, and to give within a stated period any information either on oath or verified by statutory declaration, in any way relating to the profit and loss and the production and operating costs of the business carried on by or under the control or direction of the employer. . . .".

Employers point out that this section and its prying regulations would not seem very relevant to the matter of whether or not an employer is maintaining minimum wage requirements. Saskatchewan businessmen take the view that records of profit and loss, production and operating costs are—or should be— private to the operator of a business. They fail to see why all this information would be required to enforce the legal requirements of the Minimum Wage Act.

And feeling this way about it, they speculate that the CCF has an ulterior motive. The powers under the Act, they point out, would be useful to a Socialist government competing direct-ly, or intending to compete, with private business. Using these powers it could demand access to all the books and records of a business. It would also be useful to provide the CCF with information to use in a political campaign to show the profits made by private enterprise.

The only other province in Canada which appears to have legislation similar to the Saskatchewan Minimum Wage Act (Section 9), is British Columbia. This particular section in the Saskatchewan Act matches almost word for word a similar section in the B.C. Act.

There is a section of Saskatchewan's Trade Union Act which would appear to be in conflict with the province's much publicized Bill of Rights Act, and for that matter, the Canadian Bill of Rights. This is Section 27 of the Trade Union Act, which makes it compulsory for an employee to maintain membership in a union, or join a union if he is hired by an employer who has a collective bargaining agreement in force with a certified union. In this section it is compulsory, at the request of a certified union, for an employee to join the speci-fied union or be fired.

The Saskatchewan Bill of Rights Act, Section 3, deals with the "Right to freedom of conscience". It states: "Every person and every class of persons shall enjoy the right to freedom of conscience, opinion and belief, and freedom of religious associa-tion, teaching, practice and worship."

This raises an interesting point about the regulation in the Trade Union Act which requires a worker to join a certified union or lose his job. For the sake of argument, supposing he is conscientiously opposed to joining a union because of its repu-tation, because it is Communist-led, or for some similar reason. What is his position under the two Saskatchewan Acts? If the Bill of Rights means what it says, his "right to freedom of conscience" should exempt him from joining the union and protect his job. But what about the Trade Union Act? In Saskatchewan, one might be inclined to wager that the

Trade Union Act would take precedence. Anyway, it would be a good point to raise with the Labor Relations Board.

Section 5 of the Bill of Rights Act reads: "Every person and every class of persons shall enjoy the right to peaceable assembly with others and to form with others associations of any character under the law."

By the same token, the right of association should carry with it the right of disassociation. But some of the decisions handed down by the Labor Relations Board make it fairly evident that the second right is not recognized by Saskatchewan's Trade Union Act.

Pro-union officials in the Department of Labor have been known to deliberately encourage employees to bring unfair labor charges against employers at the slightest excuse. The department also has some very efficient and fair-minded employees who take no pride in the biased behavior of the Labor Relations Board and do their best to carry out the provinces labor laws fairly and impartially.

Another gripe of private business is the way government departments regularly violate the government's Hours of Work Act, by working employees during peak work periods for longer than the prescribed eight hours per day without paying overtime. In lieu of overtime, many government employees are given time off to compensate for the extra daily time worked in any one week.

Private employers are rarely granted this concession, but instead must pay overtime rates on hours worked over certain daily limits, even though the total hours per week may well be within the limits set by law.

The entry of unions into politics as partners of the CCF in the New Democratic Party has had repercussions in the Saskatchewan Legislature. The Liberal opposition contends that Canadian union members who don't like Socialism should not be obliged to contribute political funds to the NDP by the check-off.

The Liberals tried to prevent this happening in Saskatchewan by introducing a motion at the fall session in 1961 to amend the Trade Union Act. The motion was designed to prohibit employee wage deductions from being used to finance a political party. The motion was smothered by the CCF majority.

Labor Minister Williams spoke against the motion. He denounced it as an attempt toward assuming dictatorial powers over union expenditures.

"The resolution interferes with the right of the individual to do as he pleases with his own money," said Mr. Williams, "and violates a fundamental principle of freedom. It also interferes with the right of a specific group in society to take political action."

Employers, and employees, too, who have felt the heavy hand of Saskatchewan's labor laws, might well have pointed out to Mr. Williams that the enforcement of his Trade Union Act by the Labor Relations Board violates a few fundamental freedoms, too.

In Saskatchewan today, at almost every turn, the shadow of bureaucracy intrudes between employer and employee. What has been claimed by the Socialists to be the most advanced labor legislation in Canada, is also one of the factors which has hindered and retarded the province's economic development.

10

State Medicine

THE ADVANCE OF Socialism in Saskatch-
ewan has been a nibbling process — persistent small bites
which little by little have cut into traditional rights and freedoms
enjoyed by private business and the ordinary citizen. In large
ways and little ways, the Socialists steadily move in the direction of more control over the lives of the people.

The growth of bureaucratic authoritarianism in the CCF
province has met with opposition from the Press, segments of
business and sections of the public but it remained for the
medical profession of Saskatchewan to close ranks and issue a
blunt "no" to the attempt of the Socialists to conscript doctors
in a plan of compulsory medical care insurance administered by
the government.

The Socialist government of Saskatchewan in the almost 18
years it has been in power has introduced a great deal of
controversial legislation and provoked some bitter altercations,
but no previous dispute has stretched out so long in time, none
has produced more press headlines and incited so much heated
partisanship on the part of the public as the struggle of the
doctors to resist the domination of medical services by the government.

The points at issue between the medical men and the CCF
are simple and basic. The profession will not accept the loss of
autonomy and freedom which it contends would result from a
plan controlled by the government. In the view of the doctors

the scheme the government seeks to implement provides no built-in protection against political interference, influence and control.

The government contends that the only effective way to extend medical care insurance at equitable cost to all members of the population is through compulsion and state control.

The doctors' side of the controversy has as its chief spokesman the president of Saskatchewan's College of Physicians and Surgeons, Dr. H. D. Dalgleish. The president of the 900-member College explains the doctors' position this way:

"The Saskatchewan medical profession would be remiss in its duty to the patient and to its own concept of good medicine to take any position other than one of opposition to a government invasion of personal health services which would trespass upon the established rights and freedoms of patient and doctor and inevitably lead to a decline in the quality of medical care in Saskatchewan."

The medical men of the province made it clear from the outset of the dispute that they were just as anxious as the government to make economical medical care insurance available to every citizen. They differ only with the CCF on the best methods to bring this about.

The profession proposed an alternate plan which it said would achieve the same results but eliminate the need for government compulsion and control. The doctors' proposal limited the government's role to one of providing subsidies to indigents, low-income groups and persons who because of age or pre-existing medical conditions were unable to secure coverage at nominal rates.

With the provision of financial assistance to these special categories and encouragement to self-supporting citizens to provide for their own health insurance, the doctors argued that this would do the job of extending maximum coverage to the population. The profession pointed out that this expanded programme of medical care insurance could be handled through the facilities of private prepaid insurance plans presently operating in Saskatchewan and thereby avoid the need to set up a costly government apparatus to administer a compulsory plan.

The doctors estimated the cost to the treasury of their plan at not much in excess of $3,500,000 whereas the scheme to be introduced by the government would amount to an outlay annually of $21 million or more. The profession pointedly questioned the ability of the province to carry this load at a time when the economy was showing signs of strain.

In pushing through this costly medical plan, the doctors charged, the government was ignoring the needs of other neglected areas of health service. They pointed to the problem of the mentally ill and the urgent need of modern and enlightened mental health services and facilities. They were also concerned that the excessive costs of the medical care plan would further delay government action to improve and expand obsolete and over-crowded general hospital accommodation.

The doctors' proposal was not seriously entertained by the government of Tommy Douglas. It had made up its mind to bring in a compulsory medical care programme and this was done at a special sitting of the Legislature in the fall of 1961.

Mr. Douglas presided over this session of the Legislature just long enough to see the medical care bill begin its passage through the house and then he turned the reins of government over to his successor, the Hon. Woodrow S. Lloyd.

The medical scheme was a special pet of Tommy Douglas. He carried it like a banner in the 1960 election campaign and vowed nothing would stop its progress into law so long as he had a breath left in his body. He hailed the measure as another milestone in CCF welfare legislation.

After their re-election the CCF did not appear to be in any particular hurry to implement the plan. The government apparently felt that conditions were not auspicious for a further drain on the treasury and the taxpayer. But these qualms were quickly forgotten when the New Democratic Party made its debut and the clamor began for Tommy Douglas to head it. This was the signal for the CCF government to make haste with preparations to launch the scheme.

Mr Douglas' haste to get the bill through the Legislature before he surrendered his authority of premier naturally was duly noted by those familiar with the Douglas talent for political advantage. The NDP leader was accused of ramming the medical care plan through in order to display it as another triumph of Socialism when he was on the road selling the New Democratic Party line. Mr. Douglas didn't take time to answer these charges. He was too busy conducting his coast-to-coast political safari—gunning down Capitalists, prophesying economic ruin under free enterprise and, of course, passing out the word about Saskatchewan's pioneering achievement in the field of government medical care.

The Saskatchewan Medical Care Insurance Act was made law in November, 1961. The CCF prudently took care of its financing at the same time. Some new taxes were imposed as a source of revenue for the Medical Care Insurance Fund. Twenty-eight per cent of the cost of the plan was to come from personal premiums, 50 per cent from an increase in the sales tax and 22 per cent from personal income and corporation tax increases. If Saskatchewan citizens had the notion they were getting an early Christmas gift from the government when the medical bill was passed, the idea was quickly dispelled when the CCF rendered the tax bill to pay for it.

The insurance act had a comparatively easy journey through the Legislature. The Liberals put up some token resistance but they made it clear that although they were against the compulsion in the government plan they supported the principle of universal medical care insurance.

The CCF medical care plan has had a much rougher time since it left the Legislature. A determined medical profession says it will not submit to government dictation and regimentation in the field of personal health services. The doctors make it abundantly clear that they will continue to serve their patients on the same basis as before but they will have no truck with the government plan.

A few doctors have left the province because of the situation. Other medical men have signified their intention of leaving. More will undoubtedly go if the CCF attempts to force the plan on them. The scheme was scheduled to start in January, 1962. The next starting time announced was April. When April arrived the government said the plan would definitely go into operation in July. What happens when July comes is a matter for interesting conjecture. The plan may start, but it may find itself short of doctors to keep it working.

The dispute between the profession and the government has provoked angry exchanges in the Legislature, produced many heated letters pro and con in newspapers, inspired a rash of resolutions from labor unions condemning the doctors' attitude, brought as many resolutions from other organizations supporting the doctors' position.

Liberal member Wilf Gardiner during the 1962 session of the Legislature stirred up a storm when he accused the government of organizing a smear campaign against the medical men. The Liberal charged that the government had ordered party flunkeys and organizers to marshall support for the medical plan by inducing groups and individuals friendly to the CCF to pass resolutions and flood the newspapers with letters criticizing the doctors for blocking the implementation of the plan.

While this campaign was going on, said Mr. Gardiner, Health Minister Davies was performing his role of a patient, uncritical servant of the people, courteously urging the doctors to come and talk things over with the government.

Mr. Davies was something less than courteous when he rose to deny the Liberals' charges.

Socialism is an intolerant philosophy and its followers can get pretty riled and mean when some misguided person of another political faith crassly gets in the way of their large plans for the people. One of the low blows aimed at the medical profession was delivered by the CCF party organ, The Commonwealth. The paper executed this small gem under the heading "Private Enterprise."

A photograph on the front page of the Vancouver Sun of December 23 (1961) shows private enterprise at its best. It is a picture of two rival ambulance drivers fighting. They were fighting over who was to get the business. The "business" happened to be a man lying in the street dying from bullet wounds. We don't know who won the fight, but the patient definitely lost. He died 90 minutes later.

This behavior on the part of the ambulance drivers is paralleled by the doctors in Saskatchewan, who are so concerned about their private enterprise that they would let people go without medical care rather than co-operate in a medical care plan.

This was pretty harsh treatment of a profession which through the long, hard years of the depression in Saskatchewan did its job without much hope of recompense and took pot luck with the people to whom it was ministering. The doctors have given their assurance that whatever their quarrel with the government they will continue to look after their patients.

The CCF invasion of personal health services is not a development that should have caused any surprise. It was part of the basic policy enunciated in the Regina Manifesto and it appeared again in the party's 1944 election platform. A CCF election pamphlet conveyed these tidings on health:

"The CCF will therefore set up a complete system of socialized health services with special emphasis on preventive medicine, so that you and every other resident of Saskatchewan will receive adequate medical, surgical, dental, nursing and hospital care without charge. The CCF in so doing will seek the co-operation of the medical, dental and nursing professions and all the existing health organizations of the province. The administration of these services will be placed in the hands of a strictly non-political body similar to the Board of Directors of the Saskatchewan Anti-Tuberculosis League which operates our Tuberculosis Sanitoria."

Apparently the nursing profession was to be socialized along with the doctors and the dentists. The Douglas government took its first step in the direction of state-controlled health services when it introduced a compulsory hospitalization plan in 1947. During the next decade Mr. Douglas did not have much to say about further CCF plans for a state health programme. This was taken to mean that the government had decided to leave well enough alone.

Then in a speech which had the effect of the shot that was heard around the world, Mr. Douglas cleared up any misconceptions about CCF health plans. Addressing a political meeting in the small community of Birch Hills on April 25, 1959, the premier announced that the government was planning the development of a medical care plan for Saskatchewan.

This was news to the College of Physicians and Surgeons. As a body that would be vitally affected by government intervention in the field of medical care, the college asked Mr. Douglas to explain the implications of his announcement.

The premier's reply was reassuring. He advised the College that no action would be taken by the government without the "fullest possible consultation with those most vitally concerned."

Subsequent meetings with Douglas and other communications from him convinced the College that the CCF government would not proceed with a plan that was unsatisfactory to the profession. In a letter to the College dated November 20, 1959, the premier wrote:

"I have said publicly many times that the only kind of medical care programme that will succeed is one which is eminently satisfactory both to those who give the service and to those who receive it."

And then to prove beyond a shadow of a doubt that the CCF were not up to any skulduggery, Mr. Douglas in a radio address on December 16, 1959, announced five principles which would be adhered to in planning the government's medical care programme. And the premier gave this one as the fifth principle: "The fifth principle upon which this plan will be established is that it must be in a form that is acceptable both to those providing the service and those receiving it."

In the election year, 1960, it soon became evident what the Socialists intended. Mr. Douglas' fifth principle "turned up missing". The Socialists were going into a programme of socialized medicine and the doctors could like it or lump it.

After its re-election, the Douglas government went through the motions of appointing an Advisory Planning Committee on Medical Care to investigate the field of physicians' services and make recommendations that would pave the way for legislative action. The College of Physicians and Surgeons said the terms of reference of the committee were too limiting. The doctors said the study should embrace all areas of health need and especially the plight of the mentally ill and the critical shortage of general hospital accommodation.

The government said these problems would be examined later and told the committee to get on with its job. The committee—for the most part pro-government—produced a report which, with minor differences, dovetailed handsomely with what the government had been planning to do anyway. College representatives on the committee brought in a minority report of dissent but theirs was a voice that got the attention of the government's deaf ear.

The government then proceeded to get its medical care bill ready for the Legislature. The medical profession, through the College, requested it be given an opportunity to study the bill before it was tabled in the Legislature. They were assured by the government they would have this opportunity. The Douglas government sent copies of the bill to members of the profession on the day it was tabled in the Legislature!

As the next step in the implementation of its compulsory medical care plan, the government turned its attention to the naming of a Medical Care Commission to administer the plan. The CCF pamphlet quoted earlier promised that the administration of socialized health services "will be placed in the hands of a strictly non-political body. . . ."

The CCF government's idea of a "strictly non-political body" was to appoint as chairman of the commission, T. D. Tansley, a trusty political henchman and head of the Government Finance Office. The rest of the seven-member commission were either friends or employees of the government.

This was the body that was to be set up over the province's 900 doctors and which would have the power to control and direct the practice of medicine in Saskatchewan.

One of the first things Mr. Tansley did when he took over his new office was to get off a beautifully worded letter to the College of Physicians and Surgeons. Doctors and commission could now get together, said Mr. Tansley's charming letter, and really make this fine government plan work. The chairman was vexed when the postman brought him a letter of cold rejection.

After several futile attempts to entice the College into a meeting, Mr. Tansley tried an old trick: divide and conquer. He dispatched letters to individual members of the profession suggesting they might like to talk things over with the commission. This attempt to bypass the elected representatives of the profession got short shrift from the doctors. Some of Mr. Tansley's mail may have been a little hot to handle when the replies began coming in.

A Saskatchewan employer who tried Mr. Tansley's tactic with individual members of a union would risk being hauled up in front of the government's Labour Relations Board charged with an unfair labour practice.

The doctors finally did agree to a meeting with the government but on the understanding that they would be given scope to discuss the whole broad field of health problems. The meeting turned into a series of three but out of them came nothing that was productive or fruitful. The government would not abandon its plans for a compulsory medical care programme. The profession said it would not submit to government dictation and political interference in the practice of medicine.

In the closing hours of the 1962 Legislature, less than a week after its meetings with the doctors, the government introduced a few amendments to the Medical Care Insurance Act. Health Minister Davies said they were changes of a minor nature. One amendment empowered Mr. Tansley's commission to act as legal agent for all persons covered by the plan. Insured patients would be relieved of both liability and court action for medical bills. Another amendment would establish a mediation board to settle disputes over rates of payment.

At first glance it all looked innocent enough until the lawyers took a second glance. Under the surface of the amendments, the legal people found teeth and claws that made them anything but minor. Then the storm broke. Ted Davis, editorial writer for the Liberal Regina Leader-Post, in his Banks of the Wascana column, sank his spurs into the amendments to the Medical Care Act and rode the government hard:

"The amendments are described as minor. But actually, in the opinion of lawyers unconnected with the government, they are extremely drastic—amounting in effect to conscription of the medical profession, the abrogation of its civil rights.

"At the same time, a well-authenticated report was in circulation that the government was on the verge of agreeing to work out an arrangement with the doctors for the extension of the present voluntary schemes until T. C. Douglas, the former premier and now national leader of the New Democratic Party, arrived back in Regina.

"Mr. Douglas, so this report declares, brought pressure to bear on Premier Lloyd and other members of the government to scuttle negotiations with the doctors on this basis. One of the major planks in the NDP programme is a compulsory government-controlled nation-wide medical care plan, and if the Saskatchewan government agreed to the proposed compromise with the doctors this allegedly would have kicked the props out from under the NDP campaign.

"The government then is said to have decided to break off negotiations with the Saskatchewan College of Physicians and Surgeons, and to have prepared the statement read to the legislature which in effect repudiated the undertaking that the plan to be adopted in Saskatchewan would be acceptable to those rendering medical care.

"Subsequently, after a caucus of CCF-NDP members, the amendments were drawn up to establish the medical care commission as the agent of the beneficiaries under the medical care plan and for mediation of disputes over medical bills on the terms determined by the commission.

"In the opinion of lawyers, this in effect will confer on the commission the authority by indirect ways of setting the remuneration of the doctors for the services they render.

"The government has handled the medical care affair badly from the start, under a spur to establish a compulsory government plan to provide Mr. Douglas and the NDP with a strong talking point in the impending federal election. Apparently still under this spur, the government is going to fresh extremes— beyond violating the solemn pledge to devise a medical care plan acceptable to those rendering the service—to harassing the medical profession and putting it in a straitjacket of control by the medical care commission.

"The doctors have provided Saskatchewan with a service of high quality. That must be acknowledged to their credit. They were prepared to extend present voluntary services—which have proved satisfactory to countless persons in Saskatchewan —on a basis which would have assured the continuation of this excellent service. Now, to satisfy further the insatiable appetite of Mr. Douglas and the NDP for a national campaign issue, the government contemplates a step which may be constitutional under the province's sovereign authority over property and civil rights but which is so extreme that many of the province's most competent doctors may forsake the province.

"Before it is too late, the Lloyd government should retreat from the extreme course it contemplates. Surely our democracy is not so impoverished as to preclude the working out of a satisfactory arrangement with the doctors independently of the desire of Mr. Douglas and the NDP to hold Saskatchewan's compulsory government-controlled medical care plan before the nation in the coming campaign. It is time the affairs of Saskatchewan were run for the benefit of the province and its people and not primarily to promote Mr. Douglas' political ambitions."

Health Minister Davies sharply refuted the report that Mr. Douglas had brought pressure to bear on the government. Said the health minister:

"There is not a vestige or shred of substance to this report. I categorically deny that any such overt pressure has been applied by either Mr. Douglas or the New Democratic Party. This is a slur on Mr. Douglas and the government."

In an editorial headed "Showing the Iron Fist", the Leader-Post discussed the implications of the amendments and briefly examined the health minister's categorical denial of interference by Mr. Douglas:

"The health minister is a former union official. His government is closely aligned with organized labor. Both are caught in a vise of political circumstances which must inevitably force them into conflict with the medical profession. Many in Saskatchewan, who feel they will suffer the consequences, are gathering behind the doctors. Although interference in the Saskatchewan dispute by ex-premier T. C. Douglas has been denied, the course of events at the Vancouver national convention of the Canadian Labor Congress last week (*April, 1962*) sets future policy for the Saskatchewan government from which it dare not deviate. Convention delegates unanimously approved a resolution commending the government for introducing its medical care plan. President Fred McClelland of the Saskatchewan Federation of Labor said the incoming CLC executive should assist the CCF-NDP government to defeat those opposing the plan. . . ."

And this was how matters stood in the spring of 1962. The CCF government said the plan was going into operation with or without the support of the doctors. The doctors said it would be without their support. They declared they were determined never to be merely another category of regimented civil servants; if necessary would close their offices July 1st and leave for more libertarian places. One thing was clear, the government had a political tiger by the tail and no doubt some of its harassed members were wishing T. C. Douglas would come back and claim it. But for Douglas this was no tiger. It was his crusader's white horse suddenly become a very dead horse, indeed.

11

The Oil Deals

WHEN THE DOUGLAS adherents were running for office in 1944 they worked hard to build the image of a party whose manners and morals and motivations were a grade or two better than those of run-of-the-mill politicians.

The CCF had not been in office very long before many electors began to realize that what made the Socialists superior to other political parties was better press agentry.

On the question of the CCF's record for square-dealing in the conduct of government business, Saskatchewan citizens would have mixed views.

The average citizen unaffected by political bias probably would be a little uncertain how to assess the record of the CCF for propriety of behavior in office. He would vaguely recall clangorous occasions in the Legislature when the government's probity was under attack but he would have trouble remembering what the hubbub was all about. He might finally decide that after all a little odor is not unusual around the premises of government, and give the Douglas record fairly good marks.

There are one or two spots on that record which the scrubbing of time has not been able to erase entirely. Certain alleged practices of government or government members have brought charges of wrong-doing from the opposition side but these charges never reached the point of a judicial inquiry.

One cloud that was never quite dispelled came back to hover over the government benches during the 1962 session of the

Legislature. This had to do with charges that the government engaged in under-the-table oil and mineral deals.

These charges were first aired in the House in 1950 by the Liberal member for Maple Creek, Alex Cameron. Mr. Cameron alleged that the government had been generous in making available to friends and employees of the government large tracts of potentially rich oil land. This was in the period around 1949 when private companies legitimately engaged in the business of oil exploration and development were being cold-shouldered by the CCF. In the view of the Socialists they were pirates plundering the natural resources of the people.

In a reference to the government's treat-'em-rough attitude to oil companies, Mr. Russ Brown, CCF member for Last Mountain and later minister of Industry and Information, made this comment at a political meeting in Roche Percee on October 21, 1953:

"We did frighten the oil companies a little. We set them back on their heels. They expected the same deal from us that they got from the Liberals but we said they could come in on our terms. We are not handing over our resources for the oil companies to exploit."

This was the attitude that drove the Imperial Oil Company out of Saskatchewan in the Forties. Imperial took its money and its equipment into the free enterprise climate of Alberta and there made petroleum history. It discovered the rich Leduc field and this was the start of a flow of oil revenue to the provincial treasury which any other Western province might well envy and hope to duplicate from whatever oil potential it possessed.

But Saskatchewan, in the words of Mr. Brown, was "not handing over our resources for the oil companies to exploit." Who the CCF did hand these resources over to engaged the attention of Mr. Cameron of Maple Creek and thereafter the public began to hear about the business activities in Saskatchewan of a Mr. F. C. Rhubbra of Montreal and his Gulf Securities Corporation Ltd.

Mr. Cameron in 1950 accused the government of turning over to this friend from Montreal a great chunk of Crown oil acreage which Mr. Rhubbra and his associates turned to profit-able use in deals oil companies were obliged to make with Mr. Rhubbra.

The Liberal member brought up these charges again during the 1962 session of the Legislature. The charges made ten years previously had been proven correct in the light of develop-ments that had occurred since then, Mr. Cameron asserted. He reviewed the history of the government's alleged under-the-table oil and mineral deals.

When the CCF came to power in Saskatchewan, said Mr. Cameron, two major oil companies, Imperial Oil and Bata Petroleums, were engaged in developing oil resources in the province. The CCF tried to force upon Imperial Oil a contract which the company would not agree to and it quit the province and transferred its activities to Alberta.

Bata Petroleums was a Saskatchewan company with 24,000 Saskatchewan shareholders, said Mr. Cameron. The company had drilled more than 30 wells and its discoveries included natural gas, potash and salt. The company established a gas service in the Town of Unity and started a salt plant.

"Here the government marched in, confiscated their books, locked the doors, laid a charge under the Securities Act and began an investigation," said the Liberal.

"When the smoke cleared away, Bata was exonerated of all charges, but found one million acres of its holdings had been confiscated by the government and the company had been rele-gated to a position where it couldn't borrow and was almost bankrupt."

After the government's near defeat in the 1948 election, Mr. Cameron recalled, the Douglas administration decided to soften its attitude to free enterprise and release 36 million acres of Crown land for petroleum exploration. About this time "a friend of the government," Mr. Rhubbra, with a firm called

Gulf Securities, obtained by permit and application 14 million acres of gas and oil reserves at a cost of one-tenth of a cent an acre.

"Now Mr. Rhubbra was in business," said Mr. Cameron. "He was now in the driver's seat. He said to the oil companies, 'If you want any acreage, deal with me.' The firms had to deal with him and he demanded his pound of flesh."

The Liberal said that Rhubbra demanded a 2½ per cent royalty on every dollar's worth of oil that was found anywhere on his 14 million acres and having no alternative, some companies accepted Rhubbra's terms.

Mr. Cameron reminded the Legislature that he had said in 1950 that Rhubbra stood to make millions if oil was discovered on the acreage he held. Rhubbra set up three companies— Calatta Petroleums Ltd., Philyrs Oil Co. Ltd. and Canada Oil Co. Ltd. Rhubbra's Canada Oil Co. in 1958 reported royalty income from Saskatchewan of $114,876; the following year it reported income of $153,680 and in 1960 its royalty earnings amounted to $165,932.

"I would point out," said Mr. Cameron, "that this is only one of his companies. The two other companies also share over-riding royalties. My information is that Rhubbra anticipates a return of $400,000 for the three companies from this over-riding royalty in 1962."

In his earlier reports of the deal Mr. Rhubbra arranged with the government, the Liberal member dealt with the transaction in more detail and gave some attention to government explanations of the amount of acreage acquired by Rhubbra's Gulf Securities Corporation. One of Mr. Rhubbra's associates in some of these transactions was a Harry Bronfman of Montreal.

Mr. Cameron in his 1950 report pointed out that the 14 million acres controlled by Gulf Securities in 1949 constituted nearly all the remaining acreage in Saskatchewan suitable for oil exploration. Companies genuinely interested in undertaking development work were forced to do business with Gulf Securities.

"According to information given to the Legislature," said Mr. Cameron, "Gulf Securities paid a fee of $9000 on nine million acres. After holding this for two days it was transferred to Tide Water Co. for a cash payment of $25,000 and an over-riding royalty of 2½ per cent on all gas and oil discovered in the area. In addition Gulf Securities secured an over-riding royalty on 1,550,000 acres held by Sohio Oil Co. and apparently some additional undisclosed consideration for withdrawing applications for additional acreage which was taken by Sohio. It is amazing that the CCF government permitted or participated in this kind of transaction."

The Daily Oil Bulletin of Calgary made this comment on the transaction: "Fred C. Rhubbra is wearing a smile today. The former Albertan . . . has completed the biggest deal of his life. In terms of land area, the deal is the largest yet completed in Canada. It provides a free ride on the exploration play for Fred Rhubbra and the group of small independent Canadian oil firms and individuals who originally took up the land permits."

Mineral Resources Minister Brockelbank was questioned about the deal between Gulf Securities and Sohio Oil Co. The minister denied that there had been any transaction involving permits between Gulf and Sohio.

The Liberals then asked him to explain how it came about that a map of his department of June 15, 1949, showed Gulf Securities holding permits that later found their way into Sohio's hands. Mr. Brockelbank replied that the map was not a legal document and only showed that Gulf Securities had applied for the area in question.

"Gulf Securities", the minister explained, "had applied for the concessions in May. In mid-June the company advised the department they were not interested in taking permits. Sohio made application very quickly after that."

The Liberals had a little trouble determining exactly how much oil acreage Mr. Rhubbra had received from the government. The government appeared not to be too sure of the amount itself. The first announcement of Mr. Rhubbra's acquisition came from Provincial Treasurer C. M. Fines who said Rhubbra had secured an option on 17 million acres. A map dated January, 1949, and issued by Mr. Brockelbank's department indicated Rhubbra had received 14 million acres. Mr. Brockelbank said this was an error, the amount was actually 9 million acres. In a statement to the press June 17, 1949, Mr. Brockelbank announced that Rhubbra was holding 10½ million acres.

In a radio address in March, 1952, Mr. Cameron dealt with the Rhubbra affair and commented on the difficulty the government seemed to be having in doing a little simple arithmetic to establish how much of the province's natural resources had been handed over to Rhubbra:

"Now according to Mr. Brockelbank, Mr. Fines' figure was wrong. Maps issued by his own department were wrong. His own press statement was wrong. According to Mr. Brockelbank everybody had been wrong including himself. The fact is, the whole deal smells to high heaven and all the squirming by Mr. Brockelbank or the government will not put things right."

Mr. Cameron also resurrected for another working over at the 1962 session of the Legislature the questionable operations of a company called Freeholders Oil Co.

This company, said the Liberal, was incorporated in 1950 "to acquire lands and mineral rights from freeholders and pool them". He said the idea of starting the company originated with an employee of the Department of Natural Resources, R. H. Havard. The president of the company was C. G. Broughton, "the premier's personal chore boy and CCF organizer in Weyburn constituency." Mr. Havard was appointed manager and the board of directors included the name of Cliff Thurston, later CCF member for Lumsden.

"This company then organized a host of salesmen to obtain mineral releases from the farmers," said Mr. Cameron. Havard, he pointed out, as an employee of the Department of Natural Resources had ready access to a large amount of confidential information useful to a company engaged in the business of acquiring mineral rights.

The company received excellent co-operation from the government, said Mr. Cameron. "Mr. Broughton, a valued friend, spoke to Mr. Young, registrar of the Securities Commission, and Mr. Young exempted Freeholders salesmen from having to register with the Securities Commission."

There was then some further involved business, said the Liberal, whereby the services of another company were engaged to manage the affairs of Freeholders Oil Co. The managing company turned out to be a Western Royalties Ltd. whose president was Mr. Broughton and whose manager was Mr. Havard.

In return for their management services, Havard and Broughton arranged to receive a 30 per cent interest in all mineral leases obtained from farmers and 30 per cent of the revenue from any production on freehold acreage.

"This slight consideration of 30 per cent didn't seem too much out of line," said Mr. Cameron. "Mr. Broughton later sold this slight consideration for $1 million cold cash."

Mr. Cameron said the effects of these "under-the-table deals" on the oil industry in Saskatchewan were plain.

"The major oil companies have been stung by government bureaucracy, loaded with excessive taxation and, having to carry these leeches on their backs, have thrown in the sponge."

The Liberal said exploration for gas and oil reserves in the province had ground to a virtual halt and no new gas wells had been brought into production in the past four years. The only drilling today is on proven reserves and that with but a handful of rigs.

"This lack of exploration has compelled the government to spend millions of dollars to purchase gas fields in Alberta to feed their empty gas lines," said Mr. Cameron. "To the chagrin of the CCF-NDP, if it were not for the gas obtained from C. D. Howe's Trans-Canada pipeline (built despite CCF opposition in Parliament), Saskatchewan would be sitting high and dry."

It was the same story all over again with uranium, Mr. Cameron charged. "Here again, government employees organized promotion companies and secured from the mineral resources department concessions on some of the choicest uranium areas in the north."

Mr. Cameron said these people broke no law "because the Legislative Assembly Act was changed to permit members of the Legislature to indulge in such activites. Where the law was changed to exempt the boss, it exempted the employee."

When the Liberal had finished his discourse, Mineral Resources Minister Brockelbank replied that he would "not waste time" answering the charges.

Charges of another kind in 1953 were brought against the Hon. C. M. Fines, the province's provincial treasurer. Mr. Fines was accused, along with the general manager of the Government Insurance Office, M. F. Allore, of taking "kickbacks" for directing insurance and bond business to a firm called Financial Agencies, an agent for the Government Insurance Office. Mr. Fines was minister in charge of the government office.

In May, 1952, J. O. Rawluk, a partner in Financial Agencies, swore out an affidavit which alleged that he had entered into an arrangement whereby he was to pay Fines and Allore 40 per cent of the commissions on business referred to Financial Agencies.

Mr. Rawluk alleged in his affidavit that his wife was placed on the payroll of Financial Agencies at a salary of $100 per month, that she never actually did any work for the company, and that the proceeds of her salary cheques were turned over to Fines and Allore as their share of the firm's commissions.

Walter Tucker, Saskatchewan Liberal leader at this time, received a copy of the affidavit during the 1952 election campaign. The donor apparently intended the document to be used during the campaign but Mr. Tucker felt that the seriousness of the charges called for a proper investigation. The Liberal waited for the opening of the 1953 session of the Legislature and placed the matter before the Crown Corporations Committee. The committee decided that Rawluk, Fines and Allore should be called before the committee and be examined under oath. The committee consisted of 36 members of the Legislature, 25 of them CCF and 11 Liberals.

The hearing attracted large crowds and the proceedings filled many newspaper columns. The evidence would have furnished a good plot for a Perry Mason TV story. There was the evidence of a document, "Exhibit R", on which some calculations had been worked out. Allore admitted under pressure that it was his handwriting but he denied that he had been calculating a 40 per cent "kickback" to himself and Fines. There was evidence of mysterious telephone calls which were supposed to have to do with arrangements for Mr. Fines to meet Mr. Rawluk and receive his "kickback". There was evidence given by Rawluk of a promenade along Eleventh Avenue where he was picked up in Fines' car in order to pass to Fines a sum of money in an envelope. There was testimony of devious attempts to get hold of the original affidavit in Rawluk's possession.

As an impartial hearing, the investigation by the committee was a joke. It was too heavily loaded with CCF members, among them Mr. Douglas. The premier turned in a fine, versatile performance as judge, jury and Crown prosecutor. It was obvious that he very badly wanted to play the role of executioner, too. He seldom was quiet and never partisan. His tongue gave poor Rawluk a bad time. He threatened Rawluk with court action. He made frequent mention of what he called Rawluk's "emotional and mental instability", and said Rawluk was suffering from a persecution complex. He suggested Rawluk was suffering from delusions that his telephone was being tapped, that he was being followed and that he thought he must carry a gun to defend himself. He did his best to suggest that Rawluk was a bit insane. He suggested that Rawluk be injected with a truth serum. Mr. Douglas seemed more interested in destroying Rawluk than in getting at the truth. There were a number of people in the audience who took a strong dislike to Douglas after that performance. They declared it was vindictive, not judicial.

Douglas interrupted the hearing on numerous occasions to assist witnesses who were giving testimony favorable to Fines and Allore and to interfere with witnesses whose testimony he did not like. He threatened once to expel Rawluk's counsel from the hearing. With still important evidence to be heard, some of it considered damaging to the defendants, Douglas demanded that the investigation cease and a report be produced.

The committee rendered its report. It has since been referred to as the "Douglas Report". It displayed all the bias and prejudice exhibited by Douglas during the hearing. It found that the Rawluk charges were "wholly unwarranted and unfounded". It played up sections of the evidence which were most unfavorable to Rawluk. It ignored, or lightly dismissed, evidence corroborating the charges made by Rawluk. It was a good heavy coat of whitewash.

Liberal members of the oppostion refused to accept the report. They opposed its adoption by the committee but they were outvoted by the CCF majority. The Liberals next presented a motion asking that the evidence be referred to a judicial commission consisting of a judge to be named by the Chief Justice of Saskatchewan. The CCF voted down the motion. The Liberals tried again. This time they moved a comprehensive amendment to the CCF report. The amendment was designed to get into the report important evidence which had been ignored by the CCF. The amendment suffered the same fate as the Liberals' first motion.

The Liberals continued to press for a judicial investigation of the Rawluk charges but the Douglas government would not agree to it.

And that was Saskatchewan's Rawluk Case. Allore resigned his post as general manager of the Government Finance Office and left Saskatchewan. On his way out of the province he was pinched for speeding.

Rawluk, who brought the charges and was put through the CCF mangle, found work of some kind in Regina and was heard from no more.

Hon. C. M. Fines continued to grace the office of the provincial treasurer for another seven years and then he stuffed his bonds and bank books into the saddlebags of his Cadillac and, like Allore, left the province. Mr. Fines was a young and impecunious Regina school teacher when he boarded the merry-go-round of political fortune in 1944 and forthwith became provincial treasurer. He showed an aptitude for handling money, was not dismayed by large transactions or steeply rising budgets presented in successive legislatures. His personal affairs prospering sufficiently to permit early retirement and travel abroad, Mr. Fines resigned his portfolio and his seat. He has shown a partiality for tropical climes and if Saskatchewan and its people's problems still concern him, it is not outwardly apparent. The last report on his Farouk-like exile placed him in Jamaica where he is supposed to be planning the construction of a multi-million dollar resort hotel. He is not likely to number many Socialists amongst its patrons.

12

Grief in Tommyland

T. C. DOUGLAS, since he quit his provincial post in the fall of 1961, has been a commuter. Armed with bag and brief case, he is one of the regulars welcomed aboard flights flying east or west out of Regina. His office today is of more modest proportions and located in the River Heights Shopping Centre. Tommy is an employee of the New Democratic Party now. His office, his small staff and his travelling expenses are the responsibility of the NDP.

The party is receiving good value for its money. Douglas is a top notch political salesman and he has been on the hop from one part of Canada to another ever since he took his new job. The NDP leader has lost none of his energy or drive for covering ground and taking on speaking engagements. Like Orczy's Scarlet Pimpernel, he is here, there and everywhere.

But there is a change in the Douglas who emerged from the NDP leadership convention in August, 1961, confidently proclaiming that Canadians would rally behind the new party and make it a force to be reckoned with at the next election. With the rousing speeches, spirited slogans and applause of the convention fading into the past, Douglas appears to have shed some of his earlier illusions about NDP election prospects. Observers find missing much of the decisiveness and optimism which marked the early weeks of his campaigning.

If Mr. Douglas, in the spring of 1962, had cause to be worried about the federal election situation, he had equally good cause not to like what was happening in Saskatchewan. His pet project, the medical care plan, was in trouble and it was trouble of a kind that would not help the election prospects of the NDP. What had been a dispute between the medical profession and the government was developing into a grass-roots protest as rural and urban populations began to realize that the government's medical care plan could lose them the services of valued family doctors. It was bad publicity for a politician who was stumping the country trying to persuade Canadians that Saskatchewan's Socialism was good for the rest of Canada.

Then, too, Tommy Douglas had good reason to know the political devastation that can result when a protest movement turns into an avenging force at the polls. This was the temper of the electorate in 1944 when it cast off an aged Liberal administration and replaced it with the CCF. Protest movements often catch fire over a single grievance or issue but from there on all the flaws and faults of government are exhumed and the process of finally fatal disenchantment begins.

The big issue in Saskatchewan in early 1962, was the government's compulsory medical care plan but there were signs of a larger storm brewing around the whole edifice of government and its record. Unique in the annals of prairie journalism was the political action endorsed by a group of major weekly newspapers in southwestern Saskatchewan. The publishers and editors of the papers adopted this resolution:

"Whereas there is a growing tendency on the part of the CCF government of Saskatchewan, which has the support of a minority of electors, toward more and more Socialism in its operations against the opposition of the majority of electors, it is therefore strongly recommended by the editors and publishers attending this zone meeting of the Saskatchewan Weekly News-paper Association that the weekly press of Saskatchewan take a firm stand in support of free and private enterprise at the time of the next provincial election."

Looking at the pattern of CCF government as it unfolded over the past seventeen years, it becomes apparent that the course set by the Socialists inevitably had to bring this form of government into collision with a traditional way of Canadian life which will accept change and interference by government up to a certain point and then balk.

It would appear that this point has been reached in Saskatchewan. The intrusion of bureaucracy and the threat of further intrusion in affairs which have not been the concern of government before have finally pricked the apathy of the public. The collision course of the CCF was charted by its own Socialist legislation—legislation which increasingly seeks to impose regimentation and controls over free institutions and the right to freedom of choice.

Compulsion or a heavier weight of government control are characteristics of almost every piece of major legislation enacted by the CCF since they came to power in 1944. These characteristics are present in the Trade Union Act, compulsory automobile insurance, the government hospitalization plan, the larger school unit system, the operations of the Timber Board, and in powers the government has placed in the hands of boards and commissions and other bureaucratic agencies of government.

The hospital plan, compulsory insurance and the larger school unit system are services which have proved their value and it would be a backward step to abolish them. Individually they pose no serious threat of state control but collectively and along with other government programmes of a more Socialistic nature they show the very large dimensions of the government's expanding apparatus of influence and authority.

Another prickly issue that has yet to be resolved in Saskatchewan is the government's plan to reorganize the municipalities into larger units. It was a plan the CCF were quietly moving to implement without a vote when a storm of protest boiled up in the rural areas and the government ran for cover. The county system of municipal government may have a great deal in its favour but local government officials are suspicious that it will mean a loss of autonomy and greater interference in their affairs by the provincial government.

This tendency of the Socialists to reach for autocratic power creeps into even minor amendments to legislation. Liberals at the 1962 session of the Legislature successfully blocked an attempt by the Department of Agriculture to introduce an amendment to an Act which would have given department surveyors the right to enter any land in the province without the owner's consent. After some arguments, the minister of agriculture yielded to opposition pressure and the amendment was rephrased to require surveyors to get permission before entering land.

The government's Breathalyzer Bill is another instance of a law which infringes on the rights of the individual. Many legal authorities regard it as placing undue restrictions upon persons who use or might use automobiles in the province. Under the powers of the law a police officer can require any person in charge of a motor car, or whom the police officer thinks might be in charge of a car, to accompany the officer to the police station and submit to a breath test. The purpose of the test is to determine whether the breath (and hence the blood) of the subject contains more alcohol than is considered safe for the control of an automobile. If a person refuses to submit to the test his driver's license may be suspended for a period up to 90 days. The fact that an individual might not have taken a drink at all makes no difference if he is asked to take the test. Refusal to comply with the officer's request is sufficient cause for suspension of his license.

The legislation has been condemned because, like other CCF bills, it wields the big stick over the citizen. That it may wield the stick for a socially-desirable reason is not the important thing. What is significant is that the time-honored principle of protection against self-crimination is taken away under this bill.

Persons charged with serious offences like murder or robbery are protected against self-crimination by common law and by federal law. In Saskatchewan a motorist may be compelled to submit to tests which may incriminate him, and which may be used against him if he is prosecuted. If he refuses to take the test his right to drive an automobile may be revoked.

As a measure designed to curb drunken driving, it has some merit. As a piece of legislation which encroaches on civil rights it is less palatable. The danger is that in having done this once can the government be trusted not to do it again and again?

In 1960, the CCF passed the Retailers Act. Its announced purpose was to control the use of trading stamps but it went much further in arrogating to the government unlimited control over retail establishments in the province. The bill was not proclaimed. It was described by the attorney-general as a club to be held over the heads of retailers.

The Mineral Contracts Renegotiation Act was designed to increase authority over oil companies and force them to renegotiate contracts with owners of mineral rights who wanted more compensation. The government frankly admitted that the Act was designed as a "big stick" with which to bring the oil companies to heel.

The big stick seems to have become the trademark of government in Saskatchewan. It was when they attempted to use the stick on the province's medical profession that the Socialists for the first time since they came to power ran head on into a solid wall of resistance. And now the protest is spreading and the grass-roots revolt that Mr. Douglas has reason to dread may be in process of building up.

The policy of rule by the big stick is not calculated to encourage private investment and development. Compulsion, control and the innate hostility of Socialism to free enterprise have had the effect of turning Saskatchewan into an island of economic blight in a prairie region where neighboring provinces have made tremendous progress in their industrialization.

The 17-year record of the Douglas administration in Saskatchewan as a document of progress would not make a very effective advertisement for selling the New Democratic Party to Canadians.

The people of the province have been short-changed on industrial development. The value of Saskatchewan's manufacturing output in 1960 was $400 million less than Manitoba's and under Alberta's production by $560 million.

Capital investment in manufacturing in Saskatchewan in 1960 was $19 million as compared with $104 million in Alberta and $59 million in Manitoba.

Saskatchewan has about 10,000 people employed in manufacturing. Manitoba factories employ almost 37,000; Alberta better than 30,000.

The province has had one of the smallest population increases in Canada since the end of Second World War. The population of Canada as a whole has grown by more than 51 per cent. British Columbia's population has increased 75 per cent. Alberta's growth is 63 per cent. Manitoba has added to its population by 25 per cent. Saskatchewan's increase is nine per cent.

Saskatchewan is the only province in Canada with a major forest resource and no pulp mill. Almost one-half the land area of the province is covered with timber. Forest production was at the level of 63 million cubic feet in 1944. By 1960, this production had declined to less than 24 million cubic feet.

The net debt of the province is in excess of $450 million, three times what it was in 1954. Interest payments amount to $20 million a year compared with $5 million in 1949. The interest figure of $20 million approximates the total budget of the province in 1934.

The tax squeeze is beginning to hurt and rumblings of protest constitute another unwelcome sound to government ears. The CCF government since 1944 has brought in 600 new taxes or levies and increased 600 others.

Symptomatic of the unfavorable political climate in Saskatchewan for development is the problem of unemployment. At one period during 1961 unemployment in Saskatchewan had reached the level of almost 30,000, despite the fact that the province has only a small industrial population.

The architect of the problems which plague Saskatchewan's economy today, is the man who was touring Canada in the spring of 1962 to warn Canadians that the social and economic conditions of the Thirties will come back unless they discard the old parties and accept the New Planned Economy of Socialism.

Farmers in Saskatchewan one year ago were almost convinced that the conditions of the Thirties had come back to the province. Two or three years of drought would seriously depress Saskatchewan's economy and Mr. Douglas would have a difficult time explaining how this could happen under the enlightened economic policies of Socialism.

One message the year 1962 communicated clearly: the political citadel erected in Saskatchewan by Tommy Douglas was beginning to show signs of stress and strain.